ARTIFICIAL INTELLIGENCE: RESHAPING HUMAN LIFE AND ENVIRONMENT

R VIJAYAGANTH

Made with ♥ on the Notion Press Platform
www.notionpress.com

Contents

CHAPTER ONE

Introduction

Artificial Intelligence (AI) is a rapidly evolving technology with far-reaching implications for our lives and the environment. It is transforming the way we interact with each other and our environment. AI is being used to create smarter, more efficient and safer systems, from autonomous vehicles to smart cities. AI-powered systems are increasingly being used to automate processes, reduce costs, and improve services.

AI is also being used to monitor and analyze environmental data, enabling us to better understand and manage natural resources. AI can be used to help reduce environmental impacts by identifying and predicting environmental changes. AI-powered systems can be used to monitor and analyze a range of data, from air and water quality to energy consumption.

AI can help us to detect and predict environmental problems, such as air and water pollution, and to plan and implement solutions. AI can also be used to improve the efficiency of our energy use, helping us to reduce our carbon footprint. AI can also be used to help protect wildlife and reduce the impact of climate change on ecosystems. AI-powered systems can be used to detect and monitor endangered species and to identify and track illegal activities, such as poaching.

The field of artificial intelligence (AI) has advanced tremendously in recent years and is now transforming the way humans interact with their environment. AI technologies have enabled us to create intelligent machines that can simulate human behavior and interact with the world around them. From autonomous vehicles to robotic surgery, AI has revolutionized many aspects of our lives. Here is an overview of some of the key concepts driving this transformation.

Machine Learning: Machine learning is a subset of AI that uses algorithms to “learn” from data. Machine learning is used for applications such as image recognition, speech recognition, and pattern recognition. By analyzing patterns in data sets, machines can make predictions and take actions without explicit instructions from humans.

Natural Language Processing (NLP): Natural language processing is a branch of AI that enables machines to understand the meaning of human language. NLP is used to build chatbots, voice assistants, and other applications that can understand natural language.

Robotics: Robotics is a field of engineering that deals with the design, construction, and operation of robots. Robotics applications are used in a variety of industries, such as manufacturing, healthcare, and transportation.

AI has been rapidly changing the way people and the environment interact. AI is a revolutionary technology that has the potential to reshape human life and the environment, and it is important to understand the implications of this technology so that it can be used responsibly and ethically.

AI is a technology that can be used to automate tasks, analyze data, and learn from patterns and trends. This technology can be used to automate mundane tasks, such as data entry and customer service, freeing up workers to focus on more creative tasks.

AI can also be used to analyze large amounts of data, such as analyzing medical records or environmental data, to identify patterns and come up with new insights. Finally, AI can be used to learn from past experiences and develop new strategies, such as self-driving cars or automated trading systems.

The potential of AI to reshape human life and the environment is immense. In the medical field, AI can be used to diagnose diseases more accurately, quickly analyze medical images, and even develop personalized treatments. AI can also be used to monitor the environment and identify potential risks, such as air pollution or water contamination. In the energy sector, AI can be used to optimize energy usage and develop more efficient energy systems.

1. Improve safety: AI can be used to improve safety in many aspects, from autonomous driving to improved surveillance systems. AI can be used to detect and prevent potential danger, such as through facial recognition or object detection.

2. Enhance decision-making: AI can be used to help humans make better decisions by providing insights and recommendations based on data. For example, AI can provide predictive analytics to help leaders make decisions about resource allocation or new product development.

3. Improve healthcare: AI can be used to improve the diagnosis and treatment of diseases by providing more accurate diagnosis and treatment plans. AI can also be used to monitor health data and alert medical professionals of potential issues.

4. Increase efficiency: AI can be used to automate many processes, such as customer service, marketing, and sales. This can improve efficiency and reduce costs, while freeing up humans to focus on more complex tasks.

5. Improve communication: AI can be used to enhance communication by providing natural language processing capabilities. This can enable more natural conversations between humans and computers, making communication more efficient and effective.

CHAPTER TWO

Software Developments

System Software

System software is a set of computer programs that control the functioning of the hardware and software of a computer system. It is the foundation of any computer system, providing the underlying infrastructure for all other programs and applications. It is responsible for the basic functioning of the machine, enabling communication between the various components, controlling the input and output of data, managing memory, managing system resources and managing the overall performance of the system. System software is also responsible for the security of the system, ensuring that unauthorized access to data and resources is prevented.

The development of artificial intelligence (AI) has enabled computers to perform complex tasks faster, more accurately and more efficiently than ever before. AI is reshaping the way we live, work and interact with each other. AI-driven systems have the potential to revolutionize industries, improve healthcare, reduce poverty and improve the environment.

AI can be used to automate manual processes, reduce human error and improve decision-making. AI-driven systems can learn from data and make decisions based on that data. This could help to reduce the amount of manual work required in many jobs, freeing up employees to focus on more creative tasks. AI-driven systems can also be used to improve customer service, by providing more personalized experiences.

Software Development

Software development has an undeniable capability to reshape human life and the environment. Artificial intelligence (AI) and machine learning are key components of software development and are driving the process of reshaping human life and the environment. AI relies on an integrated system of software and hardware that enables machines to learn, identify problems and make decisions on their own.

Advances in AI are changing the way people go about their day-to-day activities, from automation of mundane tasks such as household chores to providing personalized services such as healthcare and customer service. There are numerous applications of AI in fields such as autonomous cars, robotics, facial recognition, language processing, natural language understanding and machine translation.

The increasing application of AI in business processes means that the amount of data collected and analysed is growing exponentially. It has made possible novel analytical methods to identify patterns in data and offer predictive insights. AI is moving beyond intelligence augmentation to autonomous systems, allowing machines to make decisions without human input. This is revolutionizing not only the way that businesses work, but also the quality of living.

AI-based technologies are present in many aspects of our lives, such as smart homes, voice commands, smart cities and virtual assistant apps. This artificial intelligence technology is playing a major role in reshaping human life, for example through automation of mundane tasks such as vacuuming the house and making grocery shopping faster. AI can also identify patterns or trends in various datasets, providing insights that data analytics alone cannot provide.

AI is also providing a positive impact on the environment, with the development of technologies such as agricultural automation, soil and water management, energy conservation and smart cities. Through the use of Artificial Intelligence-based technologies and devices, energy consumption can be reduced or optimised and waste can be reduced or managed more efficiently. The development of AI also enables people to reduce their carbon footprint by facilitating remote work and higher energy efficiency.

In conclusion, Software Development and Artificial intelligence are playing a tremendous role in reshaping human lives and the environment. AI-based technologies can automate mundane tasks, provide highly personalised services and make predictive analytics possible, while also helping us conserve energy and reduce our carbon footprint. The potential of this field to provide sustainable solutions across various areas of human life and the environment is remarkable, and is only likely to expand further in the coming years.

Types of Artificial Intelligence

1. Reactive Machines: Reactive machines are the most basic form of AI, designed to respond quickly to external stimuli. They are not able to form memories or learn from their experiences, and can only react in predetermined

ways. Examples include IBM's Deep Blue chess computer.

2. Limited Memory: Limited memory AI systems are able to store and access information from past experiences to influence their current decisions. This allows them to learn and adjust their responses to changing circumstances. Examples include self-driving cars and Google's AlphaGo program.

3. Theory of Mind: Theory of mind AI systems are designed to understand and respond to the emotions and intentions of other agents. Examples include social robots and the virtual assistant technology used by Apple's Siri.

4. Self-awareness: Self-aware AI systems are able to form an understanding of their own identity and purpose, and can make decisions based on their own values. Examples include humanoid robots and autonomous artificial agents.

Different platforms for Artificial Intelligence (AI)

1. Machine Learning: Machine learning is a subfield of artificial intelligence (AI) that focuses on the development of computer systems that can learn from data and adapt their behavior accordingly. It is used in a variety of applications such as facial recognition, natural language processing, robotics, and more.
2. Robotics: Robotics is a branch of AI that focuses on the development of robots—autonomous machines that can interact with their environment. Robotics is used to automate tasks, reduce human labor, and increase efficiency.

3. Natural Language Processing (NLP): NLP is a subfield of AI that focuses on the development of computer systems that can understand and interpret human language. It has applications in customer service, search engines, and

natural language understanding.

4. Computer Vision: Computer vision is a subfield of AI that focuses on the development of computer systems that can recognize objects and interpret their surroundings. It has applications in facial recognition, object recognition, and more.

5. Autonomous Vehicles: Autonomous vehicles are vehicles that are capable of driving themselves without human intervention. They use AI to make decisions and navigate their environment without the need for a human driver.

Some real-life applications of Artificial Intelligence

1. Automated Medical Diagnosis: AI can be used to diagnose diseases quickly and accurately, reducing the chances of incorrect diagnoses and allowing for more efficient patient care.

2. Smart Homes: AI can be used to automate home systems such as climate control, lighting, and security, making life more efficient and secure.

3. Autonomous Vehicles: AI is being used in the development of self-driving cars, which could significantly reduce the number of traffic accidents.

4. Personal Assistants: AI-powered personal assistants such as Apple's Siri, Amazon's Alexa, and Google's Assistant can help with tasks such as scheduling appointments, ordering food, playing music, and more.

5. Robotics: AI-powered robots can be used in a variety of applications, from manufacturing to healthcare, to help with mundane tasks and reduce the risk of human error.

6. Image Recognition: AI can be used to identify objects in photos and videos, allowing for more accurate search results and better security.

7. Natural Language Processing: AI can be used to interpret natural language and generate automated responses, allowing for more efficient customer service.

Programming languages used for Artificial Intelligence

1. Python
2. Java
3. Lisp
4. Prolog
5. R 6. MATLAB
7. C++
8. JavaScript
9. Haskell
10. Scala

Artificial Intelligence and Machine Learning

Artificial Intelligence (AI) and Machine Learning (ML) are two of the most important technologies that are currently reshaping human life and environment. AI and ML are closely related and are being used in a variety of ways to improve the quality of life. From healthcare to transportation, AI and ML are being used to improve efficiency, accuracy, and safety.

AI is a broad term that encompasses the use of computers, algorithms, and software to perform tasks that traditionally required human intelligence. AI systems are designed to learn from experience, identify patterns, and make decisions autonomously. AI is being used to automate tasks, improve efficiency in various industries, and even drive cars. AI is also being used to assist with medical diagnosis, financial forecasting, and retail product recommendations.

The applications of AI and machine learning technologies are far-reaching, from healthcare to home automation. In healthcare, AI and ML are being used to diagnose and treat diseases, as well as to develop better treatments. AI is also being used to detect and diagnose cancer and other diseases in a more timely and accurate manner, as well as to detect dangerous medical conditions such as heart attacks and strokes.

In home automation, AI and ML are being used to create smart homes and connected devices that can be controlled remotely. With AI and ML, connected devices can understand user intentions and preferences and respond accordingly. For example, a smart thermostat could be programmed to adjust the temperature of the home based on the time of day and the weather outside.

In transportation, AI and ML are being used to create autonomous vehicles that can drive themselves and reduce traffic congestion, as well as to improve safety by detecting obstacles and avoiding collisions. In addition, AI and ML are being used to develop better and more efficient transportation options, such as ride-sharing services, which can reduce the number of cars on the road and help reduce environmental pollution.

ML is a subset of AI and is a type of algorithm that learns from data. ML algorithms are designed to identify patterns and make predictions without being explicitly programmed to do so. ML algorithms are used in a variety of ways, including facial recognition, object detection, natural language processing, and autonomous vehicles.

AI and ML are both being used to improve the quality of life in a variety of ways. In healthcare, AI and ML are being used to automate administrative tasks, streamline medical diagnosis, and identify potential treatments. In transportation, AI and ML are being used to reduce traffic congestion and improve safety. In retail, AI and ML are being used to personalize product recommendations and automate inventory management.

In addition to improving the quality of life, AI and ML are also being used to improve the environment. AI and ML are being used to monitor air and water quality, as well as to identify potential pollutants. AI and ML are also being used to improve energy efficiency and reduce carbon emissions.

AI and ML are also being used to improve the overall security of our lives and environment. AI and ML are being used to identify and block malicious cyber threats, as well as to identify and deter potential terrorist threats. AI and ML are also being used to improve the security of systems and networks.

Overall, AI and ML are both having a profound impact on human life and environment. AI and ML are being used to improve the quality of life, reduce environmental impacts, and improve security. As AI and ML continue to evolve, they will likely have an even greater impact on human life and environment in the future.

In conclusion, AI and ML are reshaping human life and environment in many ways. AI and ML are being used to improve healthcare, home automation, transportation, education, business operations, and cybersecurity. By making machines more intelligent and capable, AI and ML are enabling humans to do more with less effort, increasing efficiency, and improving the quality of life for everyone.

CHAPTER THREE

Characteristics of AI

AI is an ever-evolving technology that has the power to reshape human life and environment. Automation, intelligence amplification, and predictive analytics are just some of the ways in which AI reshapes human life and environment. As AI technology develops further, it will continue to reshape the way people interact with their environment, providing new opportunities to do things faster, better, and more efficiently.

Industries adopting AI technologies are benefiting from increased efficiency and productivity, as well as improved customer service and product quality. AI-driven automation helps streamline mundane tasks, freeing up time and resources to focus on higher-value activities. AI-powered techniques such as assisted decision-making and data analysis are providing invaluable insights into complex problems, helping to develop more sophisticated solutions.

From drones to driverless cars, AI-driven transportation technologies are transforming the way we travel. Autonomous vehicles are improving safety by detecting dangers and avoiding collisions. At the same time, AI is enabling more efficient and environmentally friendly modes of travel, as well as more accurate navigation systems.

AI is transforming healthcare by exponentially speeding up medical research and development. AI-driven medical imaging systems can detect diseases and abnormalities at earlier stages than ever before. Meanwhile, AI-driven robots are performing a range of precision operations, delivering people better outcomes and higher-quality care. In the manufacturing sector, AI-driven automation is dramatically increasing productivity and efficiency by automating a range of processes, from assembly lines to quality control. It is also helping to develop more sustainable production processes, leading to improved safety and reduced carbon emissions.

In addition, AI is also being used to combat global challenges, such as climate change and poverty. AI-driven analytics are providing invaluable insights into data such as meteorological records and economic trends, helping policymakers make informed decisions about policies. AI algorithms are also being used to detect and prevent crime, helping to keep communities safe.

AI is reshaping the way we live, work, and interact with each other. It is enabling groundbreaking innovation in industries ranging from healthcare and transportation to finance and manufacturing. At the same time, AI is helping tackle global challenges providing people with access to better care, improved safety, and smarter solutions. All in all, AI is revolutionizing the way we live our lives and shape our environment.

AI (Artificial Intelligence) has the potential to revolutionise the way humans live and work, by reshaping current and future experiences of human life and environment. AI could address some crucial issues of global importance, such as public health, climate change, employment and economic growth, while also helping to advance economic welfare and social wellbeing.

AI can automate mundane repetitive tasks, and quickly process large data sets to uncover valuable insight and drive better outcomes for us all. For example, AI infrastructures such as self-learning neural networks have made it easier for businesses to make faster and better informed decisions. Thanks to AI-enabled machine learning (ML) models, farming and agricultural yields have significantly increased, leading to improvements in crop and livestock production.

AI and machine learning (ML) can be used to develop innovative healthcare applications that can diagnose conditions, improve patient care and keep medical costs down, while also providing a wealth of data linked to the unique biology of each patient. Using AI and ML, strategic energy systems can be developed with the goal of slashing energy costs, reducing our carbon footprint and promoting renewable energy, while technological advances such as big data and IoT (Internet of Things) will enable us to monitor energy usage and greenhouse gas emissions in real-time.

On the social side, AI and ML can be used to tackle all sorts of issues, from unemployment to homelessness. AI-enabled robots could play a greater role in low-skill and low-wage jobs, which could open up employment opportunities and reduce the financial burden on certain sectors of the population. Moreover, AI can be used to evaluate certain living conditions, such as air and water quality, in order to minimise health risks, protect citizens from environmental hazards, and create more sustainable and sustainable cities.

Finally, AI can help bridge the digital divide by providing more access to digital services, such as online education, virtual healthcare, and banking services. AI can also be used to help amplify people's voice, as it can promote awareness on civic issues, enhanced accountability and social justice. AI can also be used to strengthen democracy and expand individual freedom, by providing increased access to information and communication platforms.In sum, AI has the potential to reshape human life and environment in remarkable ways. But it is not just the technology itself, but also how it is used, which will determine the full extent to which this potential is captured. Thoughtful deployment of AI, however, should provide immense opportunities, and benefit millions of people in remarkable ways.

Artificial Intelligence (AI) reshapes human life and environment in ways both small and large. It has an extensive range of potential applications, giving us unprecedented access to the world and our surrounding environment. AI can be used to help us better understand our surroundings, to make decisions faster, to automate physical and cognitive tasks, and to create powerful new tools. This article discusses three types of reshaping human life and environment through AI: automation, intelligence amplification, and predictive analytics.

Automation is the process of automating tasks to reduce the need for human interaction. Automation through AI technology can be used for complex tasks such as machine learning and natural language processing. Automation is found in manufacturing, assembly lines, and robotics, but it also has applications in business, healthcare, and transportation. Automation technologies, such as web crawlers, or robots can save humans time and effort. Automation can be used to detect patterns and anomalies in data and can also enhance decision-making processes.

Intelligence amplification (IA) is a process in which AI technology is used to augment human cognitive abilities. IA technologies can be used to simulate the capabilities of the human brain. This type of AI can be used for tasks such as planning and problem-solving. It can also be used to think counter-intuitively, which is beyond the scope of current AI applications. IA can help in decision-making processes, providing an objective and accurate viewpoint, as well as recommendations.

Finally, predictive analytics is the use of data to forecast potential outcomes or behaviors. Predictive analytics can be found in healthcare, finance, and other industries. Predictive analytics use machine learning models to analyze large datasets to predict customer behavior, detect fraud, or predict stock prices. This type of AI technology can also be used to identify areas of improvement in customer experience and to forecast trends.

CHAPTER FOUR

Applications

Autonomous Transportation :
The proliferation of Artificial Intelligence (AI) has led to a wide array of technological advancements that are increasingly being utilized in every field of human life. In the transportation sector, AI-powered autonomous transportation is rapidly becoming a popular alternative to traditional modes of transportation, such as cars and buses. This paper assesses the effects that autonomous transportation has on humans and the environment, discussing the ways in which AI can be leveraged to reshape aspects of both.

Autonomous transportation can help to improve the safety of public roads. Self-driving cars are equipped with sensors and computer vision algorithms to detect obstacles in the road and respond to changing environments. For instance, Tesla's Autopilot system uses data from its surrounding environment to adjust the car's speed and position to remain in its lane while avoiding collisions. This technology has already been shown to help reduce accidents, making the streets safer for everyone.

Autonomous vehicles can also offer the convenience of increased mobility. The abundance of data that is collected by autonomous cars can make it easier to plan trips and find the best route. This data can be used to identify traffic conditions and optimize routes, resulting in shorter travel times and improved efficiency when it comes to getting around. In addition, autonomous vehicles can eliminate the need for drivers, thus reducing the cost of transportation and making it more accessible to those who may not be able to afford traditional modes of transportation.

One of the primary benefits of autonomous transportation is its potential impact on the environment. Autonomous vehicles can employ efficient eco-friendly driving techniques that are not possible with manual driving. For example, Autopilot systems can minimize engine idle time and enable vans to drive in a smoother, slower fashion, improving fuel efficiency and significantly reducing emissions. Autonomous transportation can help reduce congestion and improve air quality as well, since fewer vehicles on the road also leads to fewer emissions. Additionally, autonomous vehicles can be powered by renewable energy sources such as solar or wind, further reducing their impact on the environment.

In addition to its environmental impact, autonomous transportation can also have an effect on human life. Autonomous vehicles require fewer resources than traditional cars, meaning they can save money and help alleviate poverty in some areas. This technology can also provide access to those with disabilities or limited mobility, allowing them to live more independent lives. Furthermore, autonomous technology has the potential to create new jobs by introducing additional roles to the transportation industry, such as fleet managers, ride-hailing services, etc.

From the discussion presented, it is clear that autonomous transportation can have a significant impact on the lives of humans and the environment. AI-powered autonomous vehicles offer a safer, more efficient alternative to traditional transportation methods, while simultaneously providing the potential for improved air quality, reduced emissions, and more accessible transportation. This technology can further reshape our world by creating new job opportunities and improving accessibility for those with disabilities. With the development of autonomous transportation, AI is reshaping human life and the environment for a brighter future.

AI Assistants :

AI assistants are increasingly being used to reshape our lives and environment. This technology is becoming increasingly popular as people begin to realize the many potential benefits it offers. AI assistants have the potential to improve efficiency, reduce healthcare costs, provide better customer service, and more.

An AI assistant is an artificial intelligence-based computer program that is designed to interact with humans in order to provide assistance. These AI programs can be employed to provide assistance in a variety of areas, including customer service, customer engagement, health care, retail, education, and other industries.

AI assistants are able to interact directly with customers and provide them with real-time, accurate customer service. AI customer service agents can provide customers with quick and helpful support, as well as solve problems or provide information about products and services. AI customer service agents are also able to provide personalized customer experiences, which can result in better customer retention and loyalty.

AI assistants can also be used to automate tasks and processes in healthcare. For example, AI applications can be used to aggregate data from medical records to improve patient outcomes. AI assistants can also be used to interpret medical data to detect diseases and predict treatments, as well as provide personalized healthcare advice.

AI assistants can also be used to promote better environmental health outcomes. AI-driven technologies can be used to detect and monitor air pollution, as well as track weather patterns and climate change trends. AI assistants can also analyze data to identify environmental hazards and provide advice on how to reduce the impact of such hazards on communities and the environment.

AI assistants can also be used to improve the educational experience of students. AI-driven technologies can be used to create personalized syllabi, identify individual learning trends, and generate customized curriculums that meet the needs of each student. AI assistants can also assist teachers by providing feedback on student learning, including measuring the progress and the success of each student.

Overall, AI assistants are proving to be a versatile and powerful tool that can be used to reshape our lives and environment in many positive ways. AI assistants are becoming increasingly popular as people begin to recognize the many potential benefits it offers. From customer service to healthcare to education and beyond, AI assistants are revolutionizing the way we live, work, and interact with the world around us.

Artificial Intelligence in Healthcare :

The implementation of artificial intelligence (AI) in healthcare is transforming the way patients receive care, transforming how clinical settings operate, and reshaping the environment of healthcare as a whole. There have been numerous ways that AI has already made an impact in healthcare, and the technology has the potential to be a powerful tool to help tackle some of the major issues plaguing the industry. In this essay, we will explore the current state of AI in healthcare, some of the benefits it can provide, and how its adoption is reshaping the landscape of healthcare in the future.

AI technology has already been utilized to automate certain tasks and improve productivity. This includes automating tasks such as checking vital signs, administering medications, diagnosing illnesses, and even predicting health outcomes. AI is able to carry out these tasks more quickly and accurately than humans, reducing the risk of errors and improving patient outcomes. In addition, AI can assist doctors and nurses in tracking medical records to make informed decisions about a patient's care. Furthermore, AI can be used to analyze medical data and identify potential diagnoses and treatments. This technology has the potential to provide beneficial insights that could improve patient care.

The implementation of AI in healthcare can also help reduce the costs associated with healthcare delivery. By automating certain processes and streamlining operations, healthcare providers can save time and money. In addition, AI can help reduce the need for manual labor, freeing up resources to be used for other tasks. This can help hospitals and other healthcare facilities cut operating costs and increase their efficiency.

In addition to providing cost savings and improved efficiency, AI can help improve patient outcomes by providing actionable insights that can help physicians and healthcare providers better manage patient care. AI can provide instant feedback and analysis on patient data while also significantly reducing the time and resources needed to investigate diagnoses and treatments. By leveraging AI to aggregate and analyze patient data, healthcare providers can gain an understanding of population trends, better manage chronic conditions, and more accurately predict patient outcomes.

In the future, AI could potentially revolutionize the healthcare industry by providing faster, more accurate treatments, reducing the cost of care, and empowering patients with more control over their own medical decisions. For example, AI can be used to monitor patients' vital signs and predict potential diseases or medical conditions. This could help clinicians diagnose and treat illnesses more quickly and effectively, enabling them to save time and resources. AI can also be used to provide personalized care and treatments for patients, which can help improve long-term outcomes and reduce healthcare costs.

AI is an incredibly powerful tool with the potential to dramatically transform the healthcare industry. By automating certain tasks, providing predictive analytics, and enabling personalized care, AI can help healthcare providers become more efficient, reduce the cost of care, and improve patient outcomes. As AI continues to become more advanced, it is certain to reshape the environment of healthcare. By taking advantage of its transformative power, healthcare providers can improve the quality and availability of care, making life better for patients and healthcare professionals alike.

AI-driven Education :

AI-driven education has the potential to reshape human life and environment in many ways. It can exist to assist, enhance, or completely replace traditional human instruction and teaching. AI-driven education can help in:

automating processes to make it easier, quicker, and less expensive to learn; delivering customized educational experience to each learner; and providing feedback to learners so they improve more efficiently.

Automation is one of the biggest advantages of using AI in education. AI can automate mundane and tedious tasks that take up a teacher's time and energy, making it easier and quicker to learn. Automation through the use of AI means that fewer resources are required to conduct lessons. AI could also be used to reduce administration costs, as AI-driven systems can manage courses, track assessment, award certifications, and process payments more efficiently and quickly than manual systems.

Customization is an important factor when it comes to AI-driven education. AI can be used to personalize education for each specific learner, providing a unique and tailored learning experience. AI-driven systems can track and analyze a learner's progress and use the data collected to create individualized lesson plans and materials or direct the student to resources that are suitable for their particular level of understanding. This would reduce the amount of time spent on teaching students about topics that are beyond their understanding and equip them with the skills and knowledge that they need most.

Furthermore, AI can offer feedback and guidance to learners that traditional education can't. AI can offer real-time tracking and advice on how to improve. AI-driven systems can identify areas that need improvement and provide course recommendations and other materials to help learners understand and master topics they're struggling with. This could potentially reduce the time it takes to complete an educational program, meaning that each student can learn more efficiently.

In conclusion, AI-driven education has the potential to reshape human life and environment. It can automate mundane and tedious tasks to make learning faster and more efficient, personalize lessons for each learner, and offer feedback and guidance to those who need it. AI-driven education can be immensely beneficial for both students and teachers, as it can improve the learning experience and reduce the time it takes to complete educational programs.

Robotics and AI:

Robotics and Artificial Intelligence (AI) have revolutionized human life and our environment in a multitude of ways. Robotics and AI are reshaping the way people interact with, and within, their environment. AI robotics technology is being deployed across our environment to provide us with improved services and tools to make our lives easier, safer and more efficient.

Robots are being used to create better medical treatments, which includes robotic surgery. This is a procedure that requires minimal human interaction and less invasive techniques compared to traditional methods. Robotics is also being used to create prosthetics for those with physical disabilities. Robotic prosthetics work in tandem with the human body by providing mechanical support and additional functions that would not be possible without its use. Advances in AI and robotics also allow robots to detect and respond to abnormalities in patients, providing physicians with easy-to-interpret data to better serve their patients.

AI and robotics are also being used to help improve the food industry. These tools are being used to produce more efficient, nutritious, and safer food products with increased accuracy and hygiene. From automated harvesting and detection of ripeness to automated food preparation and delivery, robots are being used to make food production and delivery more efficient and cost-effective.

Robotics and AI are also being used to increase efficiency and accuracy in the manufacturing industry. Robotics are able to automate entire processes, from assembly to painting and polishing, saving time and money due to its precise accuracy and lesser need for expensive and time-consuming manual labor. Similarly, AI is used in industrial processes and materials handling to accurately and promptly identify and process raw materials.

The use of robotics and AI in agriculture is also a powerful tool that can increase the efficiency of crop cultivation, harvesting and production. By measuring pesticide levels and water flow, detecting weeds, controlling soil moisture, and excess nutrients, robotics in agriculture can provide precise results and minimize any human error that the process is prone to.

AI and robotics can help in the conservation of our environment. These technologies enable the monitoring of data that helps to create a more efficient and sustainable use of our resources. For example, robots can be used to patrol and record pollution data in our oceans, while AI can be used to track water usage and identify potential sources of water contamination.

Robotics and AI are also helping to make our lives more convenient. Robots are being used to deliver items, act as personal assistants, and provide security for our homes. AI is being used to bring personalization to our daily lives. AI-based applications, such as app to monitor physical activity, can provide users with personalized content, such as dietary guidelines, to optimize their well-being.

The advancements in robotics and AI have shown that they present an incredible opportunity for us to shape and reshape our environment, our lifestyle, and our relationship with technology. From providing us with better medical treatments to making our lives more convenient and secure, AI and robotics have provided us with a wide range of possibilities and opportunities to expand our horizons and move into the future. By creating new opportunities and improving existing ones, robotics and AI are revolutionizing our lives, our environment, and our planet.

Data Science and Big Data :

In recent years, the technological advances in the realm of data science and big data analysis have revolutionized how enterprises and individuals leverage the knowledge from immense stores of data. This, in turn, has the potential to completely reshape our understanding of the human experience and the environment in which we live through the power of artificial Intelligence (AI).

Data science combines elements from statistics, mathematics, computer science and technology to create comprehensive data-driven models. These models extract information from vast volumes of data, often referred to as big data, and are used to create insights and predictions about our society, economy and environment. The data collected can be of various forms, ranging from human demographic information, trends in purchases and other transactional patterns, to even more granular level such as weather trends, machine-generated data and biochemical sequences. The massive growth of the internet and vast improvements in the field of communication and electronic devices have resulted in an exponential growth of data, resulting in many opportunities to develop analytical models to better understand the world around us.

AI, a branch of computer science that has seen an exponential growth in recent years, plays a critical role in data science and big data analysis. AI-driven applications leverage various advanced techniques to gain insights from data. AI algorithms can be used for predictive analysis, natural language processing and machine learning, each of which helps to uncover previously unknown patterns from data. This will allow us to make decisions, develop innovative strategies and design advanced architectures to solve complex and challenging problems.

Moreover, AI plays a profound role in data security as it can be used for anomaly detection and precision targeting. This helps organizations use data to detect fraudulent activity, prevent data breaches and malicious attacks. AI technologies can be further used to develop better cyber security systems, adapt to new attack vectors and protect users with access control measures.

Finally, data science and AI can be leveraged by governments to simplify administrative functions and increase efficiency. This analytics-driven approach will allow governments to make more informed decisions. AI can be used to detect any suspected violation of rules and regulations, determine public safety threats and improve infrastructure. Additionally, AI can help lawmakers and other stakeholders assess the situation, create targeted policies and implement them accurately to ensure greater transparency and fairness.

In conclusion, data science and AI have created a tremendous opportunity to reshape the human experience and environment in which we live. AI tools can be used to analyze immense volumes of data, increase efficiency and accuracy and make better informed decisions. This could help unlock otherwise invisible insights, uncover previously unknown patterns, enable predictive analysis and create effective cyber security systems. By leveraging the power of AI and data science, governments and enterprises can work together to develop unique solutions for large-scale challenges, improve transparency and accuracy and make informed decisions to enhance our society and environment.

Smart Cities :

The world is in the throes of a major revolution – the smart city revolution. Smart cities are leveraging new technology to better manage resources and respond to the needs of citizens. The emergence of artificial intelligence (AI) has accelerated the growth of this trend, enabling the reimagining of urban life and reshaping the environment in surprising ways.

At its core, smart cities are cities that use advanced analytics, connected technology and artificial intelligence to autonomously sense, interact and respond to people's needs. Smart cities are organized around the concept of an "internet of things" (IoT) – a network of devices, buildings and other items enabled by connected technology and able to "talk" to each other and manipulate data. Through the integration of these components, smart cities are able to provide better services, improved healthcare and energy efficiency, and enhanced public safety.

AI plays an important role in making smart cities 'smarter'. AI is used to collect and analyze data, allowing for a more comprehensive understanding of urban contexts. Connected sensors and cameras capture many different data points, helping to identify patterns and identify potential problems. This data can be used to create smarter infrastructure, such as intelligent traffic control systems that adjust signals based on traffic flow, or predictive maintenance systems that help prevent future outages.

AI can also be used to shape urban environments in more meaningful ways. For instance, AI-powered chatbots help to automate customer service by providing support to people when they need it. These bots can also be used to collect feedback from citizens on everything from traffic problems to city services. This feedback can then be used to measure and improve the quality of services. AI can also help identify solutions to environmental challenges such as poor air quality, by collecting data on air pollution levels and designing appropriate solutions.

The potential of AI-enabled smart cities to reshape the urban environment is exciting. Smart cities are already transforming the way people interact with their cities, by enhancing safety, providing better services, and improving quality of life. By leveraging the power of artificial intelligence and connected devices, these cities have the potential to create a future where people are empowered to take charge of their lives, access city services with ease, and be part of an interconnected eco-system – all made possible by their own technology. With the proliferation of smart cities, the concept of reshaping the human environment is quickly becoming a reality.

Artificial Intelligence and Cyber Security :

Artificial Intelligence (AI) and Cyber Security are two of the most important technologies of the 21st century. They are rapidly reshaping human life and environment in ways that are both beneficial and potentially dangerous. AI is transforming the way we interact with technology, while cyber security is providing a shield to protect our data and networks. Together, these technologies are enabling us to create new experiences and build a more secure, connected world.

AI is having a major impact on the way we live and work. In the workplace, AI is being used to automate tasks related to information processing, data analysis, and decision-making. This is allowing businesses to improve their efficiency and productivity. AI is also being used to develop more intelligent machines and robots, which can be used in manufacturing and other industries. In addition, AI is being used to develop virtual assistants and other intelligent agents that can help with various tasks such as scheduling, customer service, and analysis.

In the home, AI is being used to create smarter, more efficient appliances and devices. This includes internet-connected home devices such as thermostats and security systems, as well as robotic vacuum cleaners and other home robots that can help with a variety of tasks. AI is also being used to create virtual assistants that can help with tasks such as shopping and entertainment.

AI is also being used to develop smarter, more efficient transportation systems. Autonomous vehicles are becoming increasingly common, and AI is being used to develop more sophisticated navigation systems and safety features. AI is also being used to create smarter traffic and transport systems, including the use of drones and self-driving cars.

Cyber security is also playing an important role in reshaping human life and environment. As more of our lives and businesses become connected to the internet, cyber security becomes increasingly important. Cyber security is essential for protecting personal and financial data, as well as for preventing malicious attacks on networks and systems.

Cyber security is also being used to protect critical infrastructure and networks. Governments and companies are investing heavily in cyber security technology in order to protect their networks and systems from malicious actors. In addition, cyber security is being used to protect individuals from online predators and scammers.

The combination of AI and cyber security is creating a more secure and efficient world. AI is enabling us to create smarter, more efficient systems and devices, while cyber security is protecting these systems and devices from malicious actors. Together, these technologies are reshaping human life and environment in ways that are both beneficial and potentially dangerous.

In conclusion, AI and cyber security are two of the most important technologies of the 21st century. They are rapidly reshaping human life and environment in ways that are both beneficial and potentially dangerous. AI is transforming the way we interact with technology, while cyber security is providing a shield to protect our data and networks. Together, these technologies are enabling us to create new experiences and build a more secure, connected world.

a positive and lasting impact on the world, and it is up to us to ensure that it is used for good.

AI-driven Automation :

AI-driven automation is reshaping human life and environment in a range of ways. Automation has been around for decades, but AI has enabled greater automation and therefore a more powerful reshaping of human life and environment. AI-driven automation is changing how humans interact with their environment, how they make decisions, how they are monitored and controlled, and how businesses are operated.

AI-driven automation is changing the way humans interact with their environment. AI-driven automation can be used to create smarter, more efficient ways of interacting with the environment. AI-driven automation can be used to automate processes such as irrigation, crop monitoring, and pest control. AI-driven automation can also be used to predict weather patterns and make predictions about future events. This can help farmers and other business owners to make better decisions and plan for the future.

AI-driven automation is also changing how humans make decisions. AI-driven automation can be used to automate decision-making processes and make decisions more quickly and accurately. AI-driven automation can be used to identify patterns in data and make decisions based on those patterns. AI-driven automation can also be used to analyze customer data and make decisions about sales, marketing, and customer service.

AI-driven automation is also changing how humans are monitored and controlled. AI-driven automation can be used to monitor and control robots, drones, and other automated devices. AI-driven automation can be used to monitor the behavior of humans and make decisions about how they should be monitored and controlled. AI-driven automation can also be used to monitor the environment and make decisions about how to best manage it.

Finally, AI-driven automation is changing how businesses are operated. AI-driven automation can be used to automate processes such as customer service, sales, and marketing. AI-driven automation can also be used to automate processes such as inventory management, supply chain management, and financial management. AI-driven automation can also be used to analyze customer data and make decisions about how best to serve customers.

In conclusion, AI-driven automation is reshaping human life and environment in a range of ways. AI-driven automation is changing how humans interact with their environment, how they make decisions, how they are monitored and controlled, and how businesses are operated. AI-driven automation is revolutionizing the way humans interact with their environment and the way businesses are operated, making them more efficient, accurate, and cost-effective.

CHAPTER FIVE

Impacts of AI

The advent of Artificial Intelligence (AI) is reshaping human life and the environment in myriad ways. AI has emerged as a powerful transformative force that is impacting almost all aspects of our lives, from the way we work and play to the way we think and interact with one another.

AI promises to revolutionize and greatly enhance the way in which humans interact with the environment, uncovering new opportunities and challenges. It has already made a tremendous impact on various aspects of our lives, including employment, the economy, and the environment. This essay will discuss how AI is reshaping human life and the environment and will briefly discuss its implications for employment and the economy.

As AI becomes more advanced and sophisticated, it is increasingly being used to automate processes and activities. Automation is, of course, a double-edged sword; while it may provide greater efficiency and cost-savings, it can also lead to job losses as some positions become redundant. According to the International Labour Organization, globally an estimated 50-75 million jobs could be lost due to automation. In the United States, a McKinsey analysis suggests that 23% of tasks currently performed by humans may be replaced by automation. The adoption of AI technologies in the coming years is likely to accelerate the automation of jobs, which could lead to significant job losses across a range of industries.

At the same time, AI can also create new job opportunities. Many of the new jobs created by AI are ones which did not existed before and are only possible due to advances in AI technology. For example, AI is driving the growth of new job categories such as 'data scientists' and 'AI engineers'. AI is also enabling the development of 'smart factories' in which robots work alongside human operators to increase productivity and efficiency. The deployment of these technologies is likely to create new job opportunities in the manufacturing sector.

In addition to creating new job opportunities, AI can also be used to significantly enhance existing occupations and skills. For example, AI can be used to augment the abilities of healthcare workers, enabling them to diagnose diseases more accurately and in a shorter time frame. AI can also be used to help legal professionals improve their understanding of the law and make more accurate decisions. As AI technology advances, its use to enhance existing occupations is likely to become increasingly widespread.

In addition to the impacts on employment, AI is also transforming the wider economy. AI is being used to optimize the services businesses offer their customers, enabling them to better tailor their products and services to meet their customers' needs. AI is also making it easier for businesses to identify new opportunities in the marketplace and rapidly respond to changing market conditions. This is leading to the emergence of 'smart' businesses that are more agile, competitive, and successful than their traditional counterparts.

AI is also having far-reaching environmental implications. As AI technology improves, it is enabling the deployment of autonomous and self-driving vehicles, reducing the need for cars and reducing emissions caused by vehicle exhausts. AI is also being used to optimize energy consumption, enabling households to monitor their energy use and pinpoint areas where it would be most beneficial to reduce consumption. And AI is being used to help improve agricultural practices, enabling farmers to reduce the amount of water and pesticides used in farming practices.

In conclusion, AI is having a transformative impact on human life and the environment, with implications for employment and the economy. It is creating both job losses due to automation and new job opportunities, and is transforming the way businesses operate and interact with their customers. AI is also having a significant impact on the environment, enabling practices which reduce energy consumption, water usage and emissions. As AI technology continues to evolve, it is likely to have an even greater impact on our lives and the environment, providing new opportunities and challenges.

The world has gone through a rapid transformation in the past couple of decades. Technology has revolutionized our way of life, reshaping human life and environment in Artificial Intelligence (AI). AI has a significant impact on the present society, impacting all areas such as healthcare, governance, education, transportation, and much more. To understand the implications and impact of AI on society, it is important to understand the capabilities and possibilities of AI technology.

AI is a broad and rapidly advancing field of computer science and engineering, focused on creating machines and systems that can perform tasks that typically require human intelligence. AI systems are trained to think, act, and interact with humans in order to imitate human intelligence and behavior. AI improves the accuracy of decisions and interactions between humans and machines and allows for the automation of more mundane tasks, consequently reshaping human life and environment in our current era.

In healthcare, AI is capable of completing mundane tasks quickly and accurately, such as predicting patient health trends and diagnosing various medical conditions. AI-enabled medical imaging systems can detect diseases and abnormalities, while AI-powered robotic surgeries are becoming increasingly commonplace. In addition, AI can be used to improve patient outcomes by monitoring, tracking, and providing personalized treatment plans.

In governance, AI can work in synergy with governments to improve public policies. AI-enabled systems, such as an AI-powered chatbot, can be used to answer citizens' queries and provide services quickly and accurately. AI can also be used to improve decision-making processes within government departments by using machine learning to analyze large datasets and draw accurate predictions.

AI is also transforming education in schools and universities, from teaching to automated grading. AI-powered platforms can provide personalized learning experiences that better engage students and provide insights on their performance. AI can also be used to automate the grading process, providing faster and more accurate assessment of student performance on assignments or tests. For example, AI algorithms can be trained to recognize patterns and accuracies in essays in order to assess their quality and provide feedback.

At a larger scale, AI can be used to transform transportation and logistics by reducing traffic congestion and improving the efficiency of deliveries. AI-powered autonomous vehicles are already being developed, while AI-enabled navigation systems can provide route suggestions and optimized trip plans. AI can also be used to optimize warehouses, minimize energy consumption and improve the transport of goods across interconnected networks.

Overall, AI technology is reshaping society by optimizing every aspect of our lives. AI-powered technologies have the potential to improve healthcare, streamline government processes, transform education, and revolutionize transportation. As AI advances, it will become increasingly prevalent across many different fields, ultimately impacting and transforming our lives and environment.

Developing Sustainable Solutions :

With the rapid advances in Artificial Intelligence (AI) technology, it is becoming increasingly important to consider how AI can be leveraged to create sustainable solutions that reshape human life and the environment. AI has the potential to significantly reduce energy consumption and greenhouse gas emissions, improve resource management, and enable better decision making. As the world continues to grapple with climate change, resource depletion, and other pressing issues, AI can play a pivotal role in helping to create a more sustainable future.

One of the most important ways in which AI can be used to reshape human life and the environment is through energy efficiency. AI-driven analytics systems can be used to monitor and adjust energy usage in buildings, as well as to optimize the production and distribution of energy. AI can also be used to identify and reduce energy waste, reduce peak energy demand, and improve overall energy efficiency. This can be achieved by using AI-driven sensors to collect and analyze data and identify wasteful energy use, as well as by using AI-enabled software to manage and control energy production and demand. In addition, AI can be used to develop smart grid technologies which can optimize the distribution of electricity and reduce energy losses.

AI can also be used to improve resource management. AI-driven systems can be used to monitor and analyze resource usage, allowing for more efficient management of resources. This can include monitoring water usage, optimizing agricultural production, and optimizing energy production and distribution. AI can also be used to identify and reduce resource waste, as well as to identify potential resource shortages. Furthermore, AI can be used to develop and optimize systems for managing waste and recycling, as well as to develop more efficient systems for harvesting and using renewable energy sources.

In addition, AI can be used to improve decision making. AI-driven systems can be used to analyze data and generate insights and recommendations for decision makers. This can include analyzing data to identify trends and patterns, as well as providing recommendations for policy or business decisions. AI can also be used to automate decision making processes, allowing for faster and more accurate decisions.

Finally, AI can be used to improve the safety and security of the environment. AI-driven systems can be used to monitor and analyze environmental data, such as air and water quality, and identify potential threats. This can include identifying hazardous materials or activities, as well as predicting and responding to natural disasters or other environmental emergencies. Additionally, AI can be used to develop automated systems for controlling the spread of pests and diseases, as well as for monitoring wildlife populations and habitats.

Overall, AI has the potential to create significant positive impacts on human life and the environment. By leveraging AI to improve energy efficiency, resource management, decision making, and safety and security, it can help to create a more sustainable future. As the world continues to grapple with climate change and resource depletion, AI can play a crucial role in creating sustainable solutions that can reshape human life and the environment.

Adapting to the New Norm :

The introduction of Artificial Intelligence (AI) is rapidly reshaping human life and environment. AI enables people to make smarter decisions, automate mundane tasks, and do things that were previously not possible. AI is transforming industries like healthcare, finance, education, and transportation by providing solutions to previously unsolved problems. AI is increasingly being used to improve the quality of life, increase efficiency, and reduce costs.

AI is being used to solve some of the most challenging problems humanity faces, such as climate change and poverty. AI can be used to better understand the effects of climate change, analyze trends, and develop strategies to mitigate its effects. AI can also be used to improve the accuracy of predictive models for predicting floods, droughts, and other natural disasters. AI can be used to identify areas of poverty and analyze them to develop solutions that can reduce the number of people living in poverty.

AI is also being used to improve the way people interact with their environment. AI can be used to automate mundane tasks, such as scheduling appointments, streamlining customer service interactions, and personalizing experiences. AI can also be used to create virtual assistants that can answer questions and provide personalized recommendations. AI can also be used to optimize home energy use, automate transportation, and improve public safety.

AI is also being used to improve the way people work. AI can be used to automate tedious and repetitive tasks, such as data entry, so that employees can focus on more creative and productive work. AI can also be used to automate customer service interactions, allowing employees to focus on more important tasks. AI can also be used to improve the accuracy of decisions made by managers, allowing them to make more informed decisions.

AI is also being used to improve healthcare outcomes. AI can be used to analyze patient data to identify trends and develop strategies to better treat patients. AI can also be used to monitor patients and provide personalized healthcare advice. AI can also be used to automate medical tasks such as diagnoses and treatments, allowing healthcare professionals to focus on more important tasks.

AI is also being used to improve education. AI can be used to create virtual classrooms, allowing students to interact with teachers and other students from around the world. AI can also be used to create personalized learning experiences, allowing students to progress at their own pace. AI can also be used to automate administrative tasks, such as grading and record keeping, allowing teachers to focus on more important tasks.

AI is rapidly changing the world and reshaping human life and environment. AI is being used to solve some of the most challenging problems facing humanity, improve the way people interact with their environment, improve the way people work, improve healthcare outcomes, and improve education. As AI continues to evolve, it is important to recognize the potential benefits and risks associated with its use and to develop strategies to ensure that AI is used responsibly and ethically. AI has the potential to make a positive and lasting impact on the world, and it is up to us to ensure that it is used for good.

Reshaping human life and environment in AI has become a hot topic of discussion in recent years. AI has been heralded as a way to revolutionize the way we live, work, and interact with each other, and it is no surprise that this has created a great deal of excitement and optimism. However, it is important to be aware of the potential risks and disadvantages that come with reshaping human life and environment in AI.

The first potential disadvantage of reshaping human life and environment in AI is that it may lead to a reduction in human autonomy and decision-making. As AI becomes more sophisticated and widely used, it could become increasingly difficult for humans to make decisions and take initiative. AI-driven systems could take over tasks that humans have traditionally handled and make decisions on their behalf. This could lead to a loss of autonomy and a feeling of being disconnected from the world.

The second potential disadvantage is that AI-driven systems may be less reliable than humans. AI-driven systems are not perfect, and there is always the risk of errors or glitches that could lead to costly mistakes and losses. AI systems can be difficult to troubleshoot, and this could lead to delays and inconvenience for people relying on them. Also, AI-driven systems may not be able to account for all the nuances and complexities of human decision-making, leading to suboptimal results.

Another potential disadvantage of reshaping human life and environment in AI is that it could lead to job losses. As AI becomes more widely used, it could lead to the automation of certain jobs, such as manual labor or customer service. This could lead to a decrease in employment opportunities and an increase in unemployment. This could have a particularly devastating effect on low-income communities, as they are more likely to be affected by job losses due to automation.

Finally, reshaping human life and environment in AI could lead to an increase in inequality. AI-driven systems are not necessarily designed with fairness or equity in mind, and this could lead to an increase in disparities between different groups of people. AI could be used to make decisions about who gets access to resources and services, and those decisions could be biased against certain groups. This could lead to a decrease in social mobility and a widening of the gap between the haves and the have-nots.

Overall, while reshaping human life and environment in AI has the potential to revolutionize the way we live, work, and interact with each other, it is important to be aware of the potential risks and disadvantages that come with it. AI-driven systems could lead to a reduction in human autonomy, reliability problems, job losses, and an increase in inequality. It is critical to ensure that any AI-driven system is designed with fairness and equity in mind.

The introduction of artificial intelligence (AI) into human life and the environment brings with it both advantages and disadvantages. AI is a type of computer technology that is capable of performing tasks and completing complex tasks that would otherwise be too difficult or impossible for humans to do. AI has become increasingly popular in recent years, with applications in many different industries, such as healthcare, manufacturing, transportation, and finance.

Advantages of AI are many. AI can automate mundane tasks, freeing up human resources to focus on more pressing and creative endeavors. Automation can also reduce the amount of time and effort needed to complete a task, increasing efficiency and productivity. AI can also improve accuracy and reduce the chances of errors. In addition, AI can be used to detect patterns and identify trends in data, which can be used to develop new products and services.

However, there are also several disadvantages associated with AI. One of the most significant is the potential for misuse. AI can be used to manipulate, manipulate, and exploit people, leading to potential harm and abuse. AI can also be used to make decisions without human oversight, potentially leading to biased and unethical decisions. Additionally, AI can be used to monitor and track individuals, leading to privacy issues and potential security risks. Furthermore, AI can be used to create automated systems that lack flexibility and can be difficult to update or modify.

Additionally, there are ethical concerns surrounding the use of AI in human life and the environment. AI is capable of making decisions and taking actions without human input, leading to potential ethical dilemmas. There is also the potential for AI to be used to exploit people or the environment, leading to further ethical concerns. Finally, there is the potential for AI to replace or replace human workers, leading to job losses and economic disruption.

The use of Artificial Intelligence (AI) to reshape human life and environment has the potential to revolutionize the way humans live and interact with their environment. However, there are several potential disadvantages to using AI in this way. First, AI can lack the capacity to make ethical decisions and may instead act on predetermined algorithms or predetermined data. This can lead to decisions being made that are not in the best interests of humans or their environment. Second, AI can create a "black box" where it is difficult to understand the decisions that are being made. This could lead to individuals making decisions without understanding their full implications or potential consequences. Third, AI can be used to create automated systems that rely on predetermined parameters and do not take into account the complexity of human behavior or the environment. Finally, AI can be used to manipulate data and create false scenarios that lead to incorrect decisions.

The implications of using AI to reshape human life and environment can also have a negative impact on privacy and security. AI can be used to collect large amounts of data about individuals and their activities and this could lead to individuals having their privacy invaded without their knowledge or consent. Additionally, AI systems can be used to gain access to sensitive information, such as financial or medical records, which could be used for malicious purposes. Furthermore, AI can be used to create automated systems that are vulnerable to attack, which could lead to the disruption of services or the exploitation of data.

In conclusion, while the use of AI to reshape human life and environment has the potential to revolutionize the way humans live and interact with their environment, there are several potential disadvantages that need to be considered. These include the potential for AI to lack the capacity to make ethical decisions, create a "black box" where it is difficult to understand the decisions being made, invade privacy and security, create autonomous robotic systems that could lead to the displacement of human labor, and create a new "technological elite" who have access to the most advanced AI systems. It is therefore important to ensure that these potential pitfalls are taken into consideration when considering the use of AI to reshape human life and environment.

One of the most significant uses of AI in the defense sector is in the development of smart weapons systems. AI-enabled weapons systems can autonomously identify and track targets, making them more accurate and efficient than traditional weapons. This is particularly useful in unmanned aerial vehicles (UAVs), where AI-powered autopilots can autonomously fly and take action in response to changes in the environment.

AI is also being used to enhance security in the defense sector. AI-enabled security systems can detect, analyze, and respond to threats faster and more accurately than humans. This can help reduce the risk of threats such as cyber attacks, as well as enhance the effectiveness of defensive measures.

AI is also being used to improve surveillance and intelligence gathering. AI-enabled surveillance systems can observe and monitor activities in real-time, providing the military with greater situational awareness. They can also identify potential threats and provide early warning of impending danger.

The world is rapidly changing due to the advancements in technology, and Artificial Intelligence (AI) is one of the driving forces behind this transformation. AI has been utilized in many sectors, including the defense industry, in order to reshape human life and the environment.

In the defense sector, AI is being employed in a variety of roles in order to enhance security, increase operational efficiency, and reduce costs. For example, AI-based systems are being used to monitor surveillance data and detect threats in real time. AI-powered robots are being used to assist in the patrol of military bases and other sensitive areas, as well as to assist in the removal of unexploded ordnance. AI is also being used to develop and analyze intelligence data, enabling defense agencies to better understand their adversaries and make more informed decisions.

In terms of reshaping human life, AI is being utilized in the defense sector to improve the quality of life for military personnel and their families. For example, AI-powered robots are being used to perform mundane tasks, such as delivering supplies and providing medical care. This eliminates the need for human involvement and frees up personnel for more important tasks. Additionally, AI-based systems are being used to provide personnel with real-time data to inform decision-making, enabling them to make better-informed decisions in a timely manner.

When it comes to reshaping the environment, AI is being leveraged to reduce the environmental impact of defense operations. AI-powered systems are being used to improve energy efficiency, reduce waste and pollution, and monitor the environment for potential threats. AI is also being used to develop and analyze data related to climate change, helping defense agencies better understand the potential risks and prepare for them.

The defense sector is one of the most important sectors in the world and the use of Artificial Intelligence (AI) within the sector is becoming increasingly important. AI is allowing the defense sector to reshape how humans interact with the environment and with each other. AI is being used to improve security and safety, while also providing better situational awareness, faster decision making and greater accuracy.

AI is being used to improve the situational awareness of military personnel. By using AI to analyze data from multiple sources, such as satellite imagery and aerial surveillance, military personnel can gain a better understanding of their environment and the potential threats posed by adversaries. AI can also be used to identify objects and persons of interest, enabling personnel to take the appropriate measures to protect themselves and their assets.

AI is also being used to improve the accuracy of weapons systems. By using machine learning algorithms, weapons systems can be trained to accurately target enemy targets with minimal collateral damage. This is especially important in asymmetric warfare, where the enemy is using unconventional tactics to avoid detection.

Finally, AI is being used to improve the environmental sustainability of defense systems. AI can be used to analyze data from a variety of sources, including climate and weather data, to identify potential environmental risks. This data can then be used to develop strategies for reducing the environmental impact of defense systems.

Overall, AI is a powerful tool that has the potential to dramatically reshape human life and the environment in the defense sector. By using AI algorithms to improve security, safety, situational awareness, decision making, accuracy, efficiency and environmental sustainability, AI can provide a number of benefits to the defense sector.

Agricultural Sector Applications

Agriculture is an important economic sector, and its applications in artificial intelligence (AI) are rapidly reshaping human life and environment. AI applications in the agricultural sector have enabled farmers to increase crop yields, reduce costs, and improve quality and safety of goods. Farmers are now able to access and analyze data in real-time to make informed decisions on crop management and selection. AI-powered robots and drones are being used to collect data on soil health, crop growth, and pest and disease levels. This data can be used to shape a more effective and efficient farm management program.

Agriculture is an important economic sector, and its applications in artificial intelligence (AI) are rapidly reshaping human life and environment. AI applications in the agricultural sector have enabled farmers to increase crop yields, reduce costs, and improve quality and safety of goods. Farmers are now able to access and analyze data in real-time to make informed decisions on crop management and selection. AI-powered robots and drones are being used to collect data on soil health, crop growth, and pest and disease levels. This data can be used to shape a more effective and efficient farm management program.

AI has become a crucial tool in reshaping human life and the environment. In the agricultural sector, AI applications have been used to create new opportunities for farmers and increase the efficiency of production. This has been done through a range of applications, from crop monitoring and yield prediction to automation of farm processes.

The use of AI in crop monitoring has allowed for more accurate and timely predictions of crop yield. This has enabled farmers to make informed decisions about when to plant, water, and harvest their crops. AI can also be used to identify the optimal planting patterns and determine the ideal amount of water and fertilizer for the best results. Furthermore, AI can be used to detect pests and diseases, and alert farmers to their presence.

AI has also been used to automate farm processes. Automation can reduce labour costs and free up time for farmers to focus on other aspects of their business. It can also increase the efficiency of production processes, such as harvesting and planting, and reduce the risk of human errors. Automation can also be used to monitor and analyse data, such as soil and water conditions, to inform decisions about crop management.

Finally, AI can be used to improve the sustainability of agricultural production. AI can be used to detect changes in the environment and detect any potential risks posed to the land or crops. AI can also be used to monitor water usage and identify areas where water conservation measures can be implemented.

In conclusion, AI has been instrumental in reshaping human life and the environment in the agricultural sector. From crop monitoring and automation of farm processes to improving sustainability and reducing labour costs, AI applications in the agricultural sector have enabled farmers to make informed decisions and increase efficiency. As a result, AI applications in the agricultural sector have become an invaluable tool for farmers and agricultural production.

Aerospace Applications

Aerospace applications in reshaping human life and environment in Artificial Intelligence (AI) are making the world a better place for everyone. They are enabling us to solve problems faster and more accurately than ever before. From advanced medical treatments to more efficient transportation, aerospace applications are helping us to make a more sustainable future.

Aerospace applications are also helping to reshape the way we interact with our environment. For example, drones can be used to monitor air quality, as well as to detect and report on potential sources of pollution. Autonomous vehicles, such as self-driving cars, are also being deployed to reduce traffic congestion and make transportation more efficient.

In the medical field, AI-driven medical imaging technologies are being used to detect diseases more quickly and accurately than ever before. AI-driven medical treatments, such as robotic surgery and personalized treatments tailored to an individual's needs, are becoming more commonplace. AI is also being used to improve the accuracy of medical diagnostics.

Aerospace applications are also reshaping the way we experience the world from a human perspective. AI-powered virtual reality (VR) and augmented reality (AR) technologies are being used to create immersive experiences that allow us to explore virtual worlds and explore real-world environments. AI-powered chatbots are also being used to provide customer service and support, as well as to provide personalized recommendations and automated responses.

Aerospace applications in artificial intelligence (AI) are reshaping human life and the environment in a number of ways. AI has had a major impact on the way we live, work, and interact with each other. This is especially true in the field of aerospace, where advances in AI have enabled new capabilities and applications.

AI is also being used to explore space. AI-enabled spacecraft are being used to explore distant planets and asteroids, helping us to better understand our universe. AI-powered probes are also being used to map the surface of other planets and moons, as well as to identify potential resources for future exploration.

AI is reshaping the way we live, work, and interact with each other in a number of ways. In the field of aerospace, AI is being used to improve safety, efficiency, and the environment. It is also being used to explore space and to provide an enhanced experience for passengers. As AI continues to develop, it will have an ever-increasing impact on the way we live and work in the future.

Finally, AI-powered analytics are being used to better understand the complex relationships between data, as well as to improve decision-making. AI-driven analytics can also help to identify potential risks and opportunities in the marketplace. All of these applications are helping to make our lives easier, safer, and more efficient.

Overall, aerospace applications are reshaping human life and environment in AI in many ways. By leveraging the power of AI, we can solve complex problems faster and more accurately than ever before. From medical applications to transportation to immersive experiences, AI-driven technologies are making the world a better place for everyone.

AI can reduce human error

AI (Artificial Intelligence) is a rapidly evolving technology that is revolutionizing the way humans live, work, and interact with the environment. AI has the potential to reduce human error and reshape human life and environment in many ways.

Artificial Intelligence (AI) has been making strides in reshaping human life and the environment, reducing human error in a number of ways. AI can analyze large amounts of data and quickly identify patterns that are difficult for humans to spot, reducing the potential for human error. It can also automate mundane, repetitive tasks, freeing up humans to focus on more meaningful tasks and reducing the risk of error from fatigue or distraction.

AI-driven predictive analytics can help identify problems before they occur, and AI-enabled automation can reduce the need for manual labor, making industrial processes more efficient and reducing energy consumption and pollution. AI can also be used to monitor and manage water and energy resources, helping to improve conservation efforts.

In healthcare, AI is used to diagnose diseases more accurately, improve patient outcomes, and reduce medical errors. AI-driven medical devices can detect anomalies and alert doctors earlier than ever before, allowing for earlier treatment and more effective outcomes. AI-based chatbots and virtual assistants can be used to help patients better understand their medical conditions and find the right treatment.

AI can also be used to improve safety. AI-powered sensors and cameras can detect objects and alert drivers to potential hazards, reducing the risk of collisions. AI-enabled drones can be used to inspect infrastructure and detect damage, helping to identify problems before they turn into disasters. AI-driven robots can be used to explore hazardous environments and perform dangerous tasks, reducing the risk to human workers.

AI-enabled robots can also be used to help with disaster relief efforts, such as search and rescue, or to provide medical assistance in remote areas. AI-driven automation can improve agricultural production, reducing water and fertilizer use, and helping to create sustainable food systems. AI-powered robots can also be used to clean up hazardous waste and pollution, making our environment safer.

AI has the potential to revolutionize many aspects of our lives, and it has already begun to reshape human life and the environment in a number of ways. By reducing human error, AI can help make our world safer, smarter, and more sustainable.

First, AI can increase safety and reduce human error in the workplace. For example, AI can be used in factory automation to detect potential hazards and reduce the chance of workplace accidents. AI can also be used to automate mundane tasks, such as quality control, which can reduce human error and improve the quality of products. AI can also help reduce human error in healthcare by providing more accurate diagnosis and faster treatment. AI can also be used to detect fraud and reduce the risk of financial losses.

Second, AI can help make the environment cleaner and healthier. AI can be used to monitor air and water quality, identify sources of pollution, and alert authorities when action needs to be taken. AI can also help in the development of sustainable energy sources and the implementation of renewable energy sources to reduce greenhouse gas emissions. AI can also be used to automate farming and agricultural systems, reducing the need for manual labor and improving crop yields.

Third, AI can help improve human life by providing better services and information. AI can be used in transportation to reduce traffic congestion, improve public transportation, and create smart cities. AI can also be used to provide better healthcare services by analyzing medical records and providing personalized treatments. AI can also be used to improve education by providing personalized learning experiences, offering better learning resources, and creating virtual classrooms.

Finally, AI can help improve communication and relationships between humans. AI can be used to create virtual assistants that can help people manage their daily activities and communicate with others. AI can also be used to create virtual shopping experiences, providing customers with personalized recommendations and better customer service.

In conclusion, AI has the potential to improve and reshape human life and environment by reducing human error, increasing safety, improving the environment, and providing better services and information. AI can help us create a more sustainable and equitable world for everyone.

AI can work dangerous jobs

The rise of Artificial Intelligence (AI) has the potential to reshape human life and environment in a variety of ways, including by taking on dangerous jobs. AI can be used to perform hazardous tasks that would be too dangerous for a human to attempt. With AI, these tasks can be completed quickly, safely, and more efficiently than if a human were to do them.

AI can be used to explore hazardous environments, such as in deep-sea research or in disaster relief operations. AI-powered robots can enter dangerous areas and take pictures, collect data, and provide valuable information to researchers and emergency responders. AI-powered machines can also be used in hazardous industrial settings, such as in factories and mines, to make sure safety regulations are followed and that machines are functioning properly.

AI can also be used to increase the safety of dangerous jobs, such as construction, by providing real-time data on potential hazards and alerting workers to any potential risks. AI-powered drones can be used to inspect dangerous structures and provide detailed information on any potential risks, such as areas of corrosion or structural instability. This data can then be used to plan repairs or construction projects more safely and efficiently.

AI can also be used to monitor dangerous work environments to ensure that safety regulations are being followed. For example, AI-powered cameras can be used to detect any workers who are not wearing the appropriate safety gear or who are working outside of the regulated safety zone. This data can then be used to alert managers to any potential issues and help them take the appropriate steps to ensure that workers are protected from dangerous conditions.

AI can also be used to improve the safety of transportation systems. AI-powered systems can be used to monitor vehicles and alert drivers to any potential dangers. AI can also be used to analyze data from traffic cameras and other sensors to detect any potential traffic accidents or incidents. This data can then be used to improve traffic flow and reduce the risk of accidents.

AI can also be used to improve the performance of dangerous jobs, such as in the military. AI-powered systems can be used to monitor battlefields and provide real-time data to commanders. This data can be used to analyze potential threats and provide the military with the information they need to make the best decisions and protect their personnel.

AI can also be used to improve the safety of space exploration. AI-powered robots can be used to explore hazardous environments, such as on other planets, and provide scientists with valuable data that can be used to plan future missions. AI can be used to analyze the data from space probes and provide researchers with valuable insights into the structure and composition of other planets.

The advent of Artificial Intelligence (AI) has opened up a world of new possibilities, with the potential to revolutionize how humans interact with the environment and with each other. AI can be used in a variety of ways, from aiding medical treatments to helping with security and surveillance. But perhaps the most far-reaching application of AI is in the reshaping of human life and the environment.

AI can help in dangerous jobs such as mining, hazardous waste disposal, and disaster relief. AI-driven robots can work in dangerous environments, such as deep underground or in nuclear reactors, without risking human life. AI-driven robots can also be used to detect and defuse bombs in war zones, or to help with search and rescue operations.

AI can also be used to help with environmental conservation. By monitoring ecological systems and predicting changes in climate, AI can help to reduce the impact of human activities on the environment. AI-driven robots can be used to clean up oil spills, monitor air quality, and detect deforestation.

AI can also be used to improve public safety. AI-driven autonomous vehicles can be used to patrol streets and detect potential threats, while AI-driven systems can be used to detect crime patterns and alert police to suspicious activity. AI-driven facial recognition systems can be used to identify criminals and detect potential threats.

AI can also be used to improve public transportation. AI-driven autonomous vehicles can be used to reduce traffic congestion and to make public transportation safer and more efficient. AI-driven systems can also be used to improve traffic flow and reduce travel times.

AI can also be used to improve healthcare. AI-driven systems can be used to diagnose illnesses accurately and quickly, helping to reduce the risk of medical errors. AI can also be used to automate medical processes and to analyze patient data to identify potential risks and to suggest treatments.

AI can also be used to improve energy efficiency. AI-driven systems can be used to monitor energy usage in factories and homes, to detect energy waste and to suggest ways to reduce energy consumption. AI-driven systems can also be used to optimize energy production and distribution, helping to reduce the environmental impact of energy production.

Finally, AI can be used to improve the quality of life. AI-driven systems can be used to automate mundane tasks, freeing up time for people to focus on more meaningful pursuits. AI can also be used to improve education, by providing personalized learning experiences tailored to each student's individual needs.

AI has the potential to revolutionize how humans interact with the environment and with each other. By using AI to automate dangerous jobs, to conserve the environment, to improve public safety, to improve public transportation, to improve healthcare, to improve energy efficiency, and to improve the quality of life, AI can play a pivotal role in reshaping human life and the environment.

In conclusion, AI has the potential to reshape human life and environment by taking on dangerous jobs that would otherwise be too dangerous for humans. AI-powered systems can be used to explore hazardous environments, monitor dangerous work environments, and improve the safety of transportation systems. AI can also be used to improve the performance of dangerous jobs, such as in the military and space exploration. By taking on these dangerous tasks, AI has the potential to make the world a safer and more efficient place.

AI helps in repetitive jobs

In today's modern world, Artificial Intelligence (AI) is transforming the way humans interact with their environment. AI is a technology that allows machines to sense, comprehend, act, and learn in ways that mimic human behavior. AI has been used to automate and streamline many mundane and repetitive tasks, freeing up humans to focus on more complex tasks and creative pursuits.

An example of AI in action is robotic automation, which is used to replace humans in manufacturing, agriculture, and other industries. AI-powered robots are able to move and manipulate objects with precision, accuracy, and speed. This leads to increased productivity, reduced costs, and improved safety. Moreover, robots can be programmed to detect and respond to anomalies, thereby reducing the risk of human error.

Artificial Intelligence (AI) is a rapidly evolving technology that has the potential to revolutionize the way humans interact with their environment. AI has the ability to automate repetitive tasks, which can free up people's time and resources, allowing them to focus on more complex tasks that require a higher level of cognition. AI can also enable more efficient decision-making by providing insights and analysis that would otherwise not be available. In addition, AI can be used to analyze large data sets to identify patterns and trends, which can be used to inform decision-making. As AI continues to evolve and become more sophisticated, it can provide tremendous benefits to humanity, reshaping our lives and environment.

One of the most significant ways that AI can reshape human life and environment is through automation. AI can be used to automate repetitive tasks such as customer service, data entry, and even certain medical procedures. This can drastically reduce the amount of time and resources required to complete these tasks, freeing up people's time and energy to focus on more complex tasks. Automation also has the potential to increase efficiency and accuracy, as AI can be programmed to perform tasks faster and more accurately than humans. This can lead to significant cost savings, as well as improved customer service, since tasks are completed faster and more accurately.

AI can also be used to help make better decisions, as it can be used to analyze large data sets and identify patterns and trends. This can be used to inform decision-making, such as in the areas of finance, healthcare, and marketing. For example, AI can be used to analyze financial data to identify trends and correlations, which can be used to inform investment decisions. Similarly, AI can be used to analyze healthcare data and identify patterns that can help inform treatment decisions. AI can also be used to analyze marketing data and identify trends that can help inform marketing strategies.

AI can also be used to improve safety and security, as it can be used to detect anomalies and potential threats. AI can be used to monitor networks and systems for suspicious activity, as well as to identify potential threats before they become a problem. This can lead to improved safety and security, as well as improved efficiency, as threats can be identified and addressed before they become an issue.

Finally, AI can be used to improve the environment, as it can be used to monitor and analyze environmental data. This data can be used to identify patterns and trends that can help inform environmental decision-making. For example, AI can be used to monitor air quality data and identify areas where pollution levels are high, which can be used to inform decisions about where to invest in pollution control measures.

Overall, AI has the potential to revolutionize the way humans interact with their environment. It can be used to automate repetitive tasks, allowing people to focus on more complex tasks. It can also be used to analyze data and identify patterns and trends, which can inform decision-making. In addition, AI can be used to improve safety and security, as well as to monitor and analyze environmental data. As AI continues to evolve, it will continue to reshape human life and environment, providing tremendous benefits to humanity.

AI is available at all times

Artificial intelligence (AI) has the potential to revolutionize and reshape human life and the environment.

AI technologies can be used to improve healthcare, create smart cities, enhance education, and develop clean energy sources. AI can help us solve complex problems and provide us with the ability to make better decisions faster.

In healthcare, AI can be used to support healthcare professionals in their clinical decisions and to diagnose diseases more quickly and accurately. AI can also help to improve patient outcomes and reduce healthcare costs. AI-driven technologies can be used to track patient data, monitor vital signs, predict health risks, improve treatments, and to create personalized health plans. AI can also be used to speed up the drug development process, identify potential treatments, and improve clinical trial design.

AI can also be used to create smart cities. Smart cities use AI to improve the quality of life of citizens by optimizing traffic flow, improving public safety, and reducing pollution. AI-driven technologies can be used to improve urban planning, monitoring of energy consumption, and management of waste and water resources. AI can also be used to improve public transportation, reduce traffic congestion, and to provide citizens with access to real-time information.

In education, AI can be used to personalize learning, increase access to education, and develop adaptive learning systems. AI-powered technologies can be used to create personalized learning experiences, monitor student progress, and provide educational support and guidance. AI can also be used to develop virtual tutors and virtual classrooms, which can improve the educational experience for students.

In the energy sector, AI can be used to develop clean energy sources such as solar and wind power. AI-driven technologies can be used to optimize the energy grid, improve energy storage and distribution, and reduce energy waste. AI can also be used to develop smart meters and to monitor energy efficiency.

AI has the potential to revolutionize and reshape human life and the environment. AI-driven technologies can be used to improve healthcare, create smart cities, enhance education, and develop clean energy sources. AI can help us solve complex problems and provide us with the ability to make better decisions faster. The benefits of AI are numerous and far-reaching, and it is important that we continue to research and develop AI technologies to ensure that they are used responsibly and ethically.

Artificial Intelligence (AI) is the science and engineering of creating intelligent machines that can think, reason, and act autonomously. AI has the potential to revolutionize the way humans live, work, and interact with the environment.

AI has already had a major impact on society. In the medical field, AI is being used to diagnose and treat diseases, identify potential drug targets, and provide personalized healthcare. AI is also being used in transportation, with autonomous cars and drones providing efficient and safe transportation. AI is also being used in agriculture to improve crop yields and to optimize the use of resources. AI is being used in finance and banking to detect fraud and manage financial transactions, and in the retail industry to automate customer service and better understand consumer preferences.

AI is also being used in education, to create personalized learning experiences and to help identify learning paths for students. AI is being used in the legal field to help detect potential legal issues and to automate the process of contract review. AI is also being used in the energy sector to help optimize energy usage and to reduce emissions.

AI is also having an impact on the environment. AI can be used to monitor ecosystems, to detect climate change, and to optimize the use of resources. AI can also be used to develop renewable energy sources, to help reduce energy consumption, and to reduce air pollution. AI can also be used to create more efficient waste management systems, to reduce water pollution, and to help prevent the spread of disease.

AI is also being used to analyze large sets of data in order to provide insights and to develop predictive models. AI is being used to improve the efficiency of business operations and to provide actionable insights. AI is also being used to create virtual assistants, chatbots, and other interactive applications to improve customer service and to automate mundane tasks.

In conclusion, AI is transforming the way we interact with the environment and reshaping the way humans live, work, and interact with each other. AI has the potential to revolutionize the way humans live, work, and interact with the environment. AI is being used in numerous industries to improve efficiency and to provide personalized experiences. AI is also being used to help reduce emissions, to optimize energy usage, and to improve waste management systems. AI is also being used to analyze large datasets and to provide actionable insights. AI is proving to be a powerful force in reshaping human life and the environment.

AI works faster than humans

The development of Artificial Intelligence (AI) has revolutionized the way humans interact with their environment and reshaped the way humans live. AI is now capable of performing complex tasks faster, more efficiently and with greater accuracy than humans ever could. AI has the potential to revolutionize the way humans work, interact with each other, and reshape the environment.

Artificial Intelligence (AI) is revolutionizing the way we live and work. AI is capable of learning, interpreting, predicting and automating complex tasks and decisions. AI is a rapidly growing technology that is disrupting the way humans interact with the world and reshaping human life and environment.

AI is becoming increasingly powerful and efficient. It can process large amounts of data quickly and accurately, making decisions for us in the blink of an eye. AI can be used to optimize processes and make decisions faster than humans, allowing us to focus on more complex tasks. AI can automate mundane tasks, freeing up more time for creative activities and enhancing our productivity. AI can also provide insights into complex problems, such as predicting the future, diagnosing diseases and discovering new materials.

AI is also being used to improve our lives. AI-enabled robotics and automation can be used to perform dangerous or difficult tasks with greater safety and accuracy. AI-enabled systems can monitor our environment, detect and respond to potential threats, and even provide personalized care. AI can be used to assist us with shopping, making it easier to find the products we want at the best prices. AI can also be used to help us make more informed decisions, providing us with up-to-date information and tailored advice.

AI is also being used to create new experiences, entertain us, and help us stay connected. AI-enabled virtual assistants can answer our questions and provide recommendations. AI-driven video games and virtual reality experiences can make gaming more immersive and entertaining. AI-driven chatbots can provide personalized customer service and help us stay connected with friends and family.

AI is transforming our world and reshaping human life and environment. It is increasing efficiency, improving safety, and providing us with new experiences. AI is also revolutionizing the way we interact with our environment, allowing us to better understand and respond to the world around us. AI is helping us make better decisions, providing us with insights and tailored advice. AI is allowing us to do more with less and make the most of our time. AI is indeed reshaping human life and environment in a positive way.

One of the biggest advantages of AI is its ability to process vast amounts of data quickly and accurately. AI can quickly analyze large data sets and make decisions that would take humans hours or even days to make. This is especially useful in fields such as healthcare, where AI can quickly detect patterns in patient data and help doctors diagnose illnesses more quickly and accurately. AI can also be used in business to quickly analyze customer data and identify potential trends and opportunities.

AI has also had a significant impact on the way humans interact with each other. AI-powered chatbots and virtual assistants can respond to customer inquiries and provide customer support in real-time. These AI-powered assistants can also be used to provide personalized recommendations and advice for customers. This has led to more efficient customer service and improved customer satisfaction.

AI has also reshaped the way humans interact with the environment. AI-powered robots can be used to perform dangerous tasks in hazardous environments, such as cleaning up oil spills or exploring extreme terrain. AI can also be used to monitor air and water quality and detect environmental hazards. In addition, AI-powered drones can be used to monitor crops and help farmers improve crop yields.

AI is also being used to automate various tasks such as driving, manufacturing, and logistics. This automation is leading to greater efficiency and lower costs for businesses. Automation also has the potential to create new job opportunities, such as training and maintenance of AI systems.

In conclusion, AI has revolutionized the way humans interact with their environment and reshaped the way humans live. AI is capable of performing complex tasks faster, more efficiently, and with greater accuracy than humans ever could. AI is transforming the way humans work, interact with each other, and reshape the environment. AI has the potential to revolutionize the way humans live, work, and interact with each other and their environment.

AI plays a huge role in social media

AI or Artificial Intelligence is increasingly playing a larger role in social media, reshaping the way humans live and interact with the environment. AI technologies are becoming increasingly integrated into various aspects of the social media experience, from search algorithms and content filtering to user recommendations and automated responses. AI is making the social media experience more efficient, convenient, and personalized.

AI has enabled social media companies to develop more comprehensive and accurate recommendation systems, allowing users to find more relevant content and connections with other users. AI algorithms can analyze user data, such as user interactions and content preferences, to provide users with personalized recommendations. This allows users to find content that is tailored to their individual interests. AI algorithms can also be used to detect and filter out malicious content, helping to ensure a safe and secure experience for users.

AI technologies are being used in automated chatbots and messaging bots, which can provide automated customer service and respond to user queries. These bots can provide valuable help to users, such as providing customer service support, answering frequently asked questions, or providing product recommendations. AI-powered bots can help to improve customer experience and reduce customer service costs.

AI is also being used in automated advertising and marketing campaigns. With AI-powered algorithms, marketers can analyze user data and create targeted messages that are tailored to individual user preferences. AI-powered marketing campaigns can be more effective than traditional campaigns, as they are more targeted and personalized. AI-powered campaigns can also help to reduce costs, as they can be more efficient and cost-effective than traditional campaigns.

AI is also being used to help improve user experience in virtual reality (VR) and augmented reality (AR) applications. AI algorithms can help to create more immersive and interactive environments, allowing users to explore and interact with their surroundings in more realistic ways. AI can also help to improve the accuracy of

VR and AR applications, allowing for more realistic visuals and increased performance.

AI is reshaping the social media experience, making it more efficient and personalized. AI-powered algorithms can help to improve user experience, increase customer service efficiency, and reduce costs. AI is also helping to improve the accuracy and performance of virtual and augmented reality applications, making them more immersive and interactive. AI is revolutionizing the way humans interact with the environment, making social media more efficient and enjoyable for users.

AI contributes to learning

Artificial intelligence (AI) is transforming the way we live, work and interact with the world around us. AI has already had a tremendous impact on our lives, from health care to transportation, and it is only going to become more influential in reshaping our lives and environment. AI is a form of technology that is designed to mimic and enhance human abilities, such as problem solving and decision making. By using computers, AI can process vast amounts of data and identify patterns and insights that humans may not be able to detect.

AI has the potential to revolutionize a variety of industries, such as healthcare, manufacturing, finance, and security. In healthcare, AI can be used to diagnose diseases, predict medical outcomes, and provide personalized treatments. AI can also be used in manufacturing to improve efficiency and reduce costs. In finance, AI can help detect fraud and money laundering. In security, AI can be used to detect suspicious activity and protect against cyberattacks.

AI is also transforming the way we learn. AI can be used to create personalized learning experiences for students and make learning more engaging and efficient. AI can adapt to the individual needs of each student and provide personalized instructional content. AI can also help teachers identify areas of improvement and provide feedback to help students progress.

AI is also being used to develop new products and services. AI can be used to create new products and services that are tailored to the needs of customers. AI can analyze customer data to better understand their needs and develop products and services that meet their needs. AI can also be used to create new products and services that are more efficient and cost-effective.

AI is also being used to make our environment more sustainable. AI can be used to monitor air and water quality, detect pollution, and provide warnings when levels are too high. AI can also be used to reduce energy consumption and waste by monitoring building energy use and identifying opportunities for efficiency.

AI is transforming the way we live and interact with our environment. AI is being used to improve the way we learn, work, and live, and it is only going to become more influential in reshaping our lives and environment. AI is a powerful tool that can help us better understand our world and make it a better place.

AI will affect the workforce

The fourth industrial revolution is upon us and it is defined by artificial intelligence (AI). The advent of AI is a major breakthrough in technology and it has been speculated that in the next few decades, AI will reshape the way humans live and work. With the increasing capabilities of AI in the fields of healthcare, transportation, finance, communication, and more, the implications for the workforce are immense.

AI has the potential to revolutionize the way humans interact with and manage their work. AI-based technologies such as machine learning and automation are reshaping traditional workforces and replacing human labor with intelligent machines. This allows companies to improve productivity and efficiency while reducing costs. AI is also being used to automate mundane and repetitive tasks, such as data entry and customer service, freeing up workers to focus on more creative and rewarding work. Furthermore, AI is being used to increase workplace safety, by providing assistance and monitoring hazardous environments, as well as in the development of products and services.

The rise of AI will also have a significant impact on the job market. With the increased use of intelligent machines, certain jobs will become obsolete, while new ones will be created. As AI continues to improve, more and more jobs will become automated, and those jobs that can't be automated will require a more specialized skill set. This shift in the job market will require workers to stay up to date with the latest technologies and adapt to the changing landscape. Additionally, the use of AI will create opportunities for those who are willing to learn and embrace the new technologies.

AI will also alter the way humans interact with their environment. AI-driven technologies are being used in the development of smart cities, which are cities that are designed to be more efficient, safe, and sustainable. Smart cities use AI to monitor and control the environment and infrastructure, such as traffic, energy usage, and waste management. AI is also being used to improve healthcare, allowing for more accurate diagnoses and personalized treatments.

The implications of AI on the workforce are profound and far-reaching. AI has the potential to revolutionize the way humans interact with their environment and manage their work. AI-based technologies such as machine learning and automation are reshaping traditional workforces and replacing human labor with intelligent machines. Furthermore, the job market is being altered by the introduction of AI-driven technologies, creating both new opportunities and challenges. Finally, AI is being used to improve the environment and infrastructure of cities, creating more efficient and sustainable systems. Ultimately, AI will continue to shape the way humans live and work, creating a brighter and more efficient future.

AI (Artificial Intelligence) has been rapidly advancing and transforming the world around us in recent years. AI is changing the way we live, work and interact with each other. AI is being used in a variety of areas such as health care, finance, transportation, education, agriculture, and much more.

The most visible and direct impact of AI on the workforce is automation. Automation is the process of using computers and robots to perform tasks that would otherwise be done by humans. Automation has been used for decades, but with the advancement of AI technology, it has become increasingly efficient and cost-effective. It has allowed businesses to reduce costs and increase productivity, resulting in improved profits. Automation has also resulted in job displacement, as many jobs that once required human labor are now done by machines.

In addition to automation, AI has had a significant impact on the workforce in other ways. AI-driven software, such as machine learning and natural language processing, has enabled businesses to make better decisions and produce higher-quality products and services. AI-augmented tools, such as virtual assistants and chatbots, are being used to streamline processes and improve customer service. AI is also being used to identify and address problems, such as detecting fraud and detecting health-related issues.

AI is also being used to create new jobs. AI-powered tools are creating new opportunities for people to work in areas such as data science, AI engineering, and software development. AI-driven technologies are also creating new jobs in fields such as finance and healthcare.

AI is also affecting the way people live and interact with each other in a more subtle way. AI-powered tools are being used to make predictions and suggest actions, such as recommending products or services. AI-driven algorithms are also being used to personalize experiences, such as providing customized content based on user preferences. AI is also being used to create virtual assistants, such as Amazon's Alexa, which can provide helpful information, reminders, and even conduct conversations.

Overall, AI is having a major impact on the workforce and reshaping the way we live and interact with each other. AI is creating new jobs and opportunities, automating processes, and making decisions for us. AI is also making life easier and more efficient, as well as creating personalized experiences. As AI continues to evolve, it will continue to have a major impact on the workforce, reshaping human life and environment.

AI has implications for human rights

AI has the potential to reshape human life and the environment in profound ways. As AI technology advances, it will have implications for human rights and the way in which people interact with the world around them.

One of the major implications of AI is the potential for increased surveillance of people's actions. AI-based systems are capable of collecting and analyzing large amounts of data in order to predict, recognize, and track individuals' behavior. This could lead to increased surveillance of individuals' lives, potentially infringing on their right to privacy. The use of AI in surveillance could also lead to discriminatory practices and potentially create a "Big Brother" state in which individuals' rights are undermined.

AI could also lead to the automation of certain tasks, potentially leading to job losses in certain sectors and a decrease in human labor. This could lead to a decrease in the standard of living for those affected and further deepen economic inequality. In addition, AI-based systems could lead to increased labor exploitation and abuse if companies are able to exploit AI-based systems to replace human labor and suppress wages.

The use of AI could also lead to a decrease in human creativity and decision-making as AI-based systems become increasingly capable of making decisions without human input. This could limit individuals' ability to think for themselves and potentially lead to the further marginalization of minority and vulnerable groups.

The use of AI in warfare could also lead to violations of human rights. The use of AI-enabled weapons could potentially lead to increased civilian casualties and the targeting of civilians in violation of international humanitarian law. The use of AI-based surveillance systems may also be used to target and attack individuals and groups, leading to violations of their right to life.

Finally, AI could lead to a decrease in the quality of life of people living in developing countries as well as a lack of access to basic necessities. AI-based systems could be used to reduce the cost of labor in these countries and make it more difficult for people to access basic services such as healthcare and education. This could lead to an increased risk of poverty and inequality in these countries.

Overall, the implications of AI for human rights are significant and should be closely monitored as AI technology advances. It is important to ensure that any AI-based systems are developed and used in a way that respects and upholds human rights and does not lead to further marginalization of individuals or groups. It is also important for governments and other stakeholders to ensure that individuals and communities in developing countries are not negatively affected by AI-based systems and that they have access to basic services and the resources they need to improve their quality of life.

Developing "good AI" is complicated

The development of artificial intelligence has long been a topic of debate for many due to the potential implications it could have on the human race. AI has the potential to reshape human life and environment in a variety of ways, from providing medical and educational advancements to improving communication and transportation. However, developing "good AI" is complicated and requires careful consideration of ethical and moral considerations.

AI is capable of learning from its environment and can be used to make decisions and take actions without the need for human input. This could be beneficial for tasks such as healthcare, where AI can be used to diagnose diseases and provide treatments. AI could also be used to improve education, as it can be used to provide personalized learning experiences to students and help them progress more quickly. AI could also be used to improve communication and transportation, as it could be used to optimize routes and reduce travel times.

However, developing "good AI" is complicated, as it requires careful consideration of ethical and moral considerations. AI systems must be designed in a way that is both beneficial and safe for humans. AI systems must also be designed to protect against potential misuse or abuse by humans. Additionally, AI systems must be designed in a way that respects and preserves human autonomy and freedom.

AI systems must also be designed to be transparent and explainable. This is important so that humans can understand how the AI system makes decisions and can trust it to make the right decisions. Additionally, AI systems must be designed to be secure and resilient against malicious attacks.

The development of "good AI" is one of the most important and influential topics of our time. Artificial intelligence (AI) has already had a profound impact on our lives, reshaping the way we live, work, and interact with our environment. In the coming years, AI will become even more integrated into our lives, and so it is essential that we develop "good AI" that will have a positive impact on society and the environment.

At its core, "good AI" is AI that furthers the goals of humanity, rather than hindering them. This means that "good AI" should be developed with an understanding of human values, ethics, and morality. AI should be designed to help us solve problems and make life easier, rather than to create more problems. It should be designed to protect human rights and ensure that everyone can benefit from the technology.

The development of "good AI" will require collaboration between experts from multiple fields, such as computer science, engineering, and the social sciences. To ensure that AI is developed with a human-centric approach, it is important that experts across these disciplines work together to ensure that all aspects of AI development are considered, from ethical implications to the potential risks to our environment.

In addition to collaboration between experts, the development of "good AI" will also require that we consider the potential impacts of AI on our environment. AI can help us reduce emissions and increase efficiency, but it can also have a negative impact on the environment if not developed responsibly. AI should be developed with an understanding of the potential environmental impacts, and with a commitment to sustainability.

Finally, the development of "good AI" will require an understanding of the potential risks associated with AI. AI can be used for malicious purposes, and so it is important that AI is developed with privacy, security, and safety in mind. As AI becomes more advanced, it will become increasingly difficult to ensure that it is not abused, and so it is important that AI is developed with robust safeguards in place.

The development of "good AI" is a complex and challenging task, but it is essential for the future of humanity and the environment. As AI becomes more integrated into our lives, it is important that we ensure that it is developed with a human-centric approach, and with an understanding of the potential environmental and security risks. With collaboration between experts from multiple disciplines, and with a commitment to sustainability, we can ensure that AI is developed responsibly and has a positive impact on our lives and the environment.

In conclusion, developing "good AI" is complicated and requires careful consideration of ethical and moral considerations. AI has the potential to reshape human life and environment in a variety of ways, from providing medical and educational advancements to improving communication and transportation. However, AI systems must be designed in a way that is both beneficial and safe for humans and respects and preserves human autonomy and freedom. Additionally, they must be designed to be transparent and explainable and be secure and resilient against malicious attacks.

AI Can Help Improve Education Worldwide

AI has the potential to revolutionize the education system and make it more accessible to people around the world. By making use of AI, the education sector can be transformed into one that is more efficient, equitable, and cost effective. AI can help improve education by providing personalized instruction, facilitating collaboration, and making learning more interactive.

Personalized instruction is one of the main ways AI can improve education. AI can be used to develop educational content that is tailored to individual students' needs and interests. This will enable students to better understand materials and focus on the topics that are most relevant to them. AI can also be used to provide personalized feedback to students and help them better understand their mistakes. This will enable students to learn faster and more effectively.

Collaboration is another way AI can help improve education. AI can be used to facilitate collaboration between students and teachers. By providing students with access to a virtual environment, AI can enable them to interact with one another, share ideas, and work together to solve problems. AI can also be used to provide guidance and support to teachers, enabling them to better understand their students' needs and provide more effective instruction.

Finally, AI can make learning more interactive. AI can be used to create interactive learning environments that can be adapted to different learning styles. AI can also be used to develop virtual simulations, allowing students to learn in a more immersive and engaging way. This will make learning more enjoyable and effective for students.

Overall, AI has the potential to revolutionize the education system and make it more accessible to people around the world. By providing personalized instruction, facilitating collaboration, and making learning more interactive, AI can help improve education worldwide. In addition, AI can help reduce costs and improve equity in education by providing students with access to high quality learning resources regardless of their location or economic status. In this way, AI can reshape human life and environment by making education more accessible and equitable for all.

Artificial Intelligence Brings About Automation

Artificial Intelligence (AI) is the science of developing intelligent machines that can think, learn, and act for themselves. It is a powerful tool for reshaping the human life and environment. AI enables machines to interpret large amounts of data, identify patterns, and make decisions with minimal or no human intervention. AI-based systems have been used to improve the efficiency of operations in various sectors, such as healthcare, finance, transportation, and energy.

AI has been a major force in reshaping human life and environment. AI-based systems have been used to improve the efficiency of operations in various industries. In the healthcare sector, AI-based systems have helped automate mundane tasks, such as data entry and record-keeping. AI can also be used to diagnose diseases and plan treatments. AI-based systems can identify patterns in patient data and improve accuracy in diagnostics. In the finance sector, AI-based systems can be used to automate investment decisions and identify potential trading opportunities. AI-based systems can also be used to automate customer service and understand customer preferences.

AI can also be used to improve the efficiency of transportation systems. AI-based systems can be used to identify potential traffic jams and plan routes for vehicles. AI-based systems can also be used to predict the demand for certain types of transportation and plan routes accordingly. Additionally, AI-based systems can be used to identify potential safety hazards and provide safety alerts.

AI can also be used to optimize energy consumption. AI-based systems can be used to analyze energy consumption data and identify ways to reduce energy consumption. Additionally, AI-based systems can be used to identify potential energy sources and predict energy demands. AI-based systems can also be used to automate the operations of power plants and monitor energy consumption.

AI can also be used to improve the efficiency of manufacturing processes. AI-based systems can be used to automate the production process and identify potential problems in the production process. AI-based systems can also be used to optimize the use of raw materials and reduce wastage. Additionally, AI-based systems can be used to analyze product data and identify areas for improvement.

AI can also be used to improve the efficiency of agriculture. AI-based systems can be used to identify potential crop diseases, optimize irrigation systems, and analyze soil data. AI-based systems can also be used to predict weather patterns and identify potential weather-related risks. Additionally, AI-based systems can be used to automate the operations of farms and monitor crop yields.

In conclusion, AI has been a major force in reshaping the human life and environment. AI-based systems have been used to automate mundane tasks in various sectors, such as healthcare, finance, transportation, and energy. AI-based systems can also be used to optimize energy consumption, improve the efficiency of manufacturing processes, and improve the efficiency of agriculture. AI-based systems can also be used to identify patterns in data and make decisions with minimal or no human intervention. AI is a powerful tool for reshaping the human life and environment and will continue to be so in the future.

AI benefit the economy

Artificial intelligence (AI) has the potential to reshape human life and the economy. AI is a set of computer algorithms that enable machines to think and act like humans, allowing them to learn and adapt to changing conditions. AI can be used in a variety of industries to automate processes, improve efficiency, and reduce errors. AI can also be used to make decisions and provide insights to businesses.

AI has the potential to improve economic performance. AI can increase productivity by automating mundane tasks such as data entry and customer service. This can free up human labor to focus on higher value tasks, such as innovation and problem solving. AI can also help businesses better understand their customers and tailor services to meet their needs. AI algorithms can analyze customer data to identify patterns and trends, allowing businesses to create more targeted marketing campaigns and products.

AI can also help reduce costs. Automation can reduce labor costs and help businesses become more efficient. AI can also be used to detect fraud and reduce errors, resulting in lower operating costs. AI can also be used to optimize supply chains, increasing efficiency and reducing costs.

AI can also improve the quality of life for individuals. AI can automate tedious tasks in the home and workplace, freeing up time for leisure activities. AI can also be used to improve healthcare. AI algorithms can help diagnose diseases, predict treatment outcomes, and suggest personalized treatments. AI can also be used to predict traffic patterns and recommend routes to reduce travel time.

AI can also help protect the environment. AI can be used to monitor and analyze data from sensors in the environment to identify potential problems. AI can also be used to optimize energy use, reduce waste, and identify areas of improvement.

AI can also have a positive impact on the economy by reducing inequality. AI can be used to detect bias in decision-making, helping to reduce discrimination and increase access to opportunities. AI can also be used to automate mundane tasks, allowing low-income workers to focus on higher value tasks that can lead to better wages.

Finally, AI can create new job opportunities. AI can create new roles, such as data scientists and AI engineers. AI can also generate new products and services, creating further employment opportunities.

Overall, AI has the potential to reshape human life and the economy. AI can increase productivity, reduce costs, improve quality of life, protect the environment, reduce inequality, and create new job opportunities. In order to take full advantage of AI, businesses and individuals must be willing to invest in the technology and adopt the necessary measures to ensure it is used responsibly.

Misconceptions about Artificial Intelligence

When it comes to Artificial Intelligence (AI), there are many misconceptions about how it can reshape human life and the environment. AI is a form of technology that involves machines that can "think" and learn, but it is not a replacement for human thought or creativity. AI can be used to improve the way humans interact with the world around them, but it is not the answer to all of humanity's problems.

One of the most common misconceptions about AI is that it will replace humans in the workplace. Although AI can be used to automate certain tasks and improve efficiency, it cannot replace the creativity and decision-making capabilities of humans. AI is simply a tool that can help humans to do their jobs more effectively.

Another misconception about AI is that it is a perfect solution for all problems. AI is still in its early stages and has a long way to go before it can be considered a perfect solution for any situation. It is important to remember that AI is only as good as the data it is given, and this data requires careful consideration and analysis before it can be used effectively.

Some people also assume that AI is the same as robots or automation. While AI can be used to control robots and automate certain processes, it is not the same as these technologies. AI is a form of artificial intelligence that is designed to "think" and make decisions, while robots and automation are simply programmed to do a specific task.

Finally, some people assume that AI will lead to the end of human life as we know it. This is simply not true. AI has the potential to improve our lives in many ways, such as helping us to make better decisions, understanding our environment, and even predicting the future. But it is important to remember that AI is a tool, and it cannot replace the power of human thought and creativity.

In conclusion, AI has the potential to reshape human life and the environment in many ways. But it is important to be aware of the misconceptions about AI and to understand that it is not a perfect solution for all of life's problems. AI is a powerful tool that can be used to improve our lives, but it should never be used as a replacement for human thought and creativity.

Computer Vision

Computer Vision in AI is the field of artificial intelligence that focuses on using computers to interpret and process visual data from the environment. It is used to create systems that can identify and understand objects in images, videos, and live footage. Computer Vision in AI is becoming increasingly important for a variety of applications, from autonomous vehicles to facial recognition and medical imaging.

Computer Vision in AI has the potential to revolutionize human life and the way we interact with the environment. By leveraging the power of AI, Computer Vision can help machines better understand their surroundings and interact with humans. This technology can be used to automate everyday tasks, diagnose medical conditions, and assist with navigation. It can enable robots to safely navigate the environment and interact with humans. Computer Vision in AI can also be used to improve safety in public spaces, such as airports and hospitals.

Computer Vision in AI can be used to detect and identify objects in real-time. This technology can be used to create automated systems that can recognize faces and objects, detect motion and activity, and distinguish between different types of objects. For example, facial recognition software can be used to quickly and accurately identify people, while object recognition can be used to identify objects in an image or video.

Computer Vision in AI can also be used to identify patterns and trends in data. This technology can be used to detect anomalies and outliers in data, helping to detect potential fraud and other suspicious activities. It can also be used to identify trends in customer behavior, helping to improve customer service and increase customer satisfaction.

Computer Vision in AI can also be used to improve the accuracy of medical diagnoses. By using computer vision to analyze medical images, doctors can better identify and diagnose medical conditions. This technology can also be used to detect disease in the early stages, helping to improve patient outcomes.

Computer Vision in AI has the potential to revolutionize the way we interact with the environment. By leveraging the power of AI, Computer Vision can help machines better understand their surroundings and interact with humans. This technology can be used to automate everyday tasks, diagnose medical conditions, and assist with navigation. It can enable robots to safely navigate the environment and interact with humans. Computer Vision in AI can also be used to improve safety in public spaces, such as airports and hospitals.

In addition to its potential to improve human life and the environment, Computer Vision in AI also has the potential to reduce costs and save time. Automated systems can process data and images more quickly than humans, helping to reduce the amount of time and money required for manual tasks. Automated systems can also reduce the risk of human error, helping to reduce costs associated with mistakes.

Computer Vision in AI is revolutionizing the way we interact with the environment and improving the quality of life. By leveraging the power of AI, Computer Vision can help machines better understand their surroundings and interact with humans. This technology can be used to automate everyday tasks, diagnose medical conditions, and assist with navigation. It can enable robots to safely navigate the environment and interact with humans. Computer Vision in AI can also be used to improve safety in public spaces, such as airports and hospitals.

Bayesian networks

Bayesian networks are a form of probabilistic graphical models used to represent a variety of complex relationships among variables. They are used in a wide variety of applications, ranging from medical diagnosis to predicting traffic flow. Bayesian networks are a powerful tool for modeling and understanding the world around us, and they are being used to reshape human life and environment in a variety of ways.

One way that Bayesian networks are being used is to improve healthcare. Bayesian networks can be used to provide better diagnoses and treatments, as they can take into account many different factors, such as the patient's medical history, current symptoms, and test results, to arrive at a more accurate diagnosis. They can also be used to identify correlations between different variables in order to determine which treatments are most likely to be successful. This can help to reduce the cost of medical treatments, as well as improve patient outcomes.

Bayesian networks are also being used to improve decision-making in business and government. By taking into account multiple factors, such as market trends, customer preferences, and economic factors, Bayesian networks can help organizations make more informed decisions. This can lead to better strategies, improved efficiency, and increased profits.

In the field of environmental science, Bayesian networks are being used to better understand the causes and effects of climate change. By considering multiple factors, such as temperature, carbon dioxide levels, and ocean currents, Bayesian networks can help to identify correlations between different variables and predict how climate change will affect different parts of the world. This can help inform policy decisions, as well as help to better prepare for the effects of climate change.

Finally, Bayesian networks are being used to improve the security of critical infrastructure, such as power grids, dams, and transportation systems. By taking into account factors such as weather conditions, population density, and security protocols, Bayesian networks can help to identify potential threats and take proactive measures to better protect these vital systems.

Overall, Bayesian networks are a powerful tool for understanding and modeling complex relationships among variables. They are being used to improve healthcare, business, environmental science, and security, among other areas. As their use continues to expand and improve, they will continue to reshape human life and environment in a variety of ways.

Reinforcement learning

Reinforcement learning (RL) is an area of artificial intelligence (AI) that has the potential to reshape human life and environment. At its core, RL is a type of machine learning (ML) that focuses on teaching an AI agent how to make decisions in order to achieve a desired goal. RL algorithms learn from interactions with the environment, and are designed to maximize rewards and minimize punishments.

RL can be used in various ways to reshape human life and environment. For example, RL can help optimize decision-making in complex systems such as traffic management or energy management. By using RL algorithms to learn from past experiences, these systems can become more efficient, reliable, and cost-effective.

RL can also be used to develop autonomous robots that can interact with the environment and learn from their experiences. Autonomous robots can be used in a variety of scenarios, such as search-and-rescue missions, warehouse automation, or even for entertainment and leisure. For example, autonomous robots can be used to explore and map unknown areas, assist the elderly with everyday tasks, or even provide companionship.

In addition, RL can be used to develop intelligent agents that can learn to interact with humans. These agents can be used in virtual assistants or chatbots to provide personalized services and advice. Intelligent agents can also be used in medical diagnosis and treatments, or to provide personalized financial advice.

Finally, RL can be used to develop artificial intelligence (AI) that can interact with the environment in a safe and responsible manner. AI can be used to improve the efficiency of manufacturing processes, automate transportation systems, or even monitor and manage the environment. By using RL to develop AI agents, we can ensure that these agents are able to take into account the potential consequences of their actions, and act in a way that is beneficial to both humans and the environment.

Overall, RL is a powerful tool that has the potential to reshape human life and environment in a variety of ways. By using RL algorithms to learn from past experiences, agents can be developed that are able to make decisions in a safe and responsible manner. In addition, RL can be used to develop autonomous robots, intelligent agents, and artificial intelligence (AI) that can interact with the environment in a safe and responsible manner. All of these applications of RL have the potential to improve our lives in a variety of ways, making RL one of the most promising areas of artificial intelligence.

Types of agents are there in Artificial Intelligence

Artificial Intelligence (AI) is a rapidly growing field of computer science which is revolutionizing the way humans interact with the world. AI has the potential to reshape human life and environment in ways never before imagined. AI is a broad term that encompasses a variety of different types of agents, each designed to perform a specific task or set of tasks.

The most common type of AI agent is the software agent, which is programmed to carry out pre-defined tasks.

These tasks can range from simple things like sorting a list, to more complex tasks like playing chess or driving a car. Software agents are very versatile in that they can be used to automate a variety of tasks across many different domains. Some examples of software agents include robots, chatbots, natural language processing (NLP) systems, and computer vision systems.

Another type of AI agent is the hardware agent, which is a physical device embedded with AI technology. Hardware agents can be autonomous, meaning they are capable of performing a task without any human input. Examples of hardware agents include drones, robots, and self-driving vehicles.

A third type of AI agent is the cognitive agent, which is an AI system that is capable of learning and adapting to its environment. This type of agent is used in tasks that require intelligent decision making, such as facial recognition, object recognition, and language translation. Cognitive agents are also used in systems that employ machine learning technology, such as search engines and recommendation systems.

A fourth type of AI agent is the social agent, which is a system that is designed to interact with humans. Social agents are used in applications such as customer service chatbots, virtual assistants, and social media bots. These agents are designed to understand and respond to human input, and to simulate human behavior.

Finally, a fifth type of AI agent is the robotic agent, which is a physical robot designed to interact with its environment. Robotic agents are used in a variety of tasks, such as manufacturing, logistics, and medical applications. This type of agent is often used in combination with software agents to increase efficiency and accuracy.

In conclusion, there are five main types of AI agents – software agents, hardware agents, cognitive agents, social agents, and robotic agents. Each of these agents has the potential to reshape human life and environment in powerful ways. By leveraging the power of AI, humans can automate mundane tasks, increase efficiency, and even make decisions that were previously impossible.

Different domains/Subsets of AI

AI (Artificial Intelligence) is a broad and ever-evolving field of computer science that encompasses many different disciplines and applications. AI is used in many aspects of life, from healthcare to entertainment, to help automate tasks and increase productivity. AI has the potential to reshape human life and the environment in numerous ways, from improving safety and security, to providing more efficient services, to reducing environmental impact.

1. Automation & Robotics: Automation and robotics are used to automate repetitive tasks, such as manufacturing and assembly line production, thereby freeing up human labor for more meaningful work. Automation and robotics can also be used to improve safety and security, as well as reduce environmental impact by reducing energy consumption.
2. Natural Language Processing (NLP): NLP is a branch of AI that focuses on understanding and generating natural language. It is used in many applications, such as chatbots, virtual assistants, and automated customer service. NLP has the potential to improve the customer experience, reduce customer service costs, and increase efficiency.
3. Computer Vision: Computer vision is a branch of AI that focuses on understanding and interpreting visual

information. Computer vision is used in many applications, such as facial recognition, object recognition, and autonomous navigation. Computer vision can be used to improve safety and security, as well as reduce environmental impact by reducing energy consumption.

4. Machine Learning: Machine learning is a branch of AI that focuses on building systems that can learn from data without being explicitly programmed. Machine learning is used in many applications, such as image and speech recognition, autonomous driving, and medical diagnosis. Machine learning has the potential to improve safety and security, as well as reduce environmental impact by reducing energy consumption.
5. Data Mining & Analysis: Data mining and analysis is a branch of AI that focuses on extracting and analyzing data from large datasets. Data mining and analysis is used in many applications, such as marketing, fraud detection, and predictive analytics. Data mining and analysis can be used to improve decision-making, reduce costs, and increase efficiency.
6. Knowledge Representation & Reasoning: Knowledge representation and reasoning is a branch of AI that focuses on representing and reasoning about knowledge. It is used in many applications, such as natural language processing, robotics, and autonomous agents. Knowledge representation and reasoning can be used to improve safety and security, as well as reduce environmental impact by reducing energy consumption.
7. Intelligent Agents: Intelligent agents are computer systems that can learn from and interact with their environment. Intelligent agents are used in many applications, such as autonomous robots and virtual

assistants. Intelligent agents can be used to improve safety and security, as well as reduce environmental impact by reducing energy consumption.

Overall, AI has the potential to reshape human life and the environment in numerous ways. AI can improve safety and security, reduce energy consumption, and increase efficiency. By leveraging the various domains of AI, we can create a better future for both humans and the environment.

Intelligent agents in AI

An intelligent agent is a computer program or piece of software that is designed to act on behalf of a human user in order to achieve a certain goal. The agent is designed to interact with its environment, to make decisions, and to act on those decisions in order to achieve its goals. In Artificial Intelligence (AI), intelligent agents are used to carry out tasks such as problem-solving, decision-making, learning, and planning.

The intelligent agent is the cornerstone of AI and has been used in a variety of applications, including robotics, healthcare, finance, and marketing. The agent is designed to mimic human behavior, to observe and interact with its environment, to make decisions and take action based on those decisions. It is also designed to autonomously learn from its environment and use the information it obtains to improve its decision-making capabilities.

In the context of reshaping human life and environment, an intelligent agent can be used to automate processes, to optimize resource utilization, and to monitor and control environmental conditions. In healthcare, for example, an intelligent agent can be used to monitor a patient's vital signs and alert a physician when there is a change in the patient's condition. In finance, an intelligent agent can be used to monitor stock prices and execute trades based on market conditions. In marketing, an intelligent agent can be used to analyze customer data to determine the best way to target customers and increase conversion rates.

The intelligent agent can also be used to automate mundane tasks such as scheduling, data entry, and customer service. This can help to free up human resources and allow them to focus on more complex tasks. Automating mundane tasks can also help to reduce costs and increase efficiency.

In the future, intelligent agents will continue to become more sophisticated and will be used in a variety of fields. For example, in the field of robotics, intelligent agents can be used to automate tasks and eliminate the need for human intervention. In healthcare, intelligent agents can be used to automate diagnosis and treatment processes. In finance, intelligent agents can be used to monitor stock prices and execute trades based on market conditions. In marketing, intelligent agents can be used to analyze customer data to determine the best way to target customers and increase conversion rates.

The potential for intelligent agents to reshape human life and environment is immense. By automating processes and optimizing resource utilization, intelligent agents can help to reduce costs and increase efficiency, allowing humans to focus on more complex tasks. Moreover, intelligent agents can help to improve decision-making, allowing humans to make more informed decisions. As AI continues to evolve, intelligent agents will continue to become more sophisticated and will have an even greater impact on our lives and the environment.

CHAPTER SIX

Conclusion

In conclusion, Artificial Intelligence has had a profound impact on human life and behavior. Over the past few decades, AI technology has advanced rapidly, revolutionizing the way humans interact with technology, and providing us with countless new tools and insights. AI has enabled us to automate mundane tasks, allowing us to focus on more intellectually challenging endeavors. AI has also allowed us to better understand and predict human behavior, and to identify patterns in data that were previously unrecognized. AI has also allowed us to create more powerful and sophisticated systems, such as intelligent robots, self-driving cars, and virtual personal assistants. Despite its many benefits, AI also poses a number of ethical challenges. For example, AI systems can be biased or inaccurate, leading to unfair outcomes and unequal access to resources. AI can also be used to automate or replace human labor, leading to job displacement and economic upheaval. Additionally, AI can be used for surveillance and other intrusive activities, which raise serious privacy concerns. Finally, AI poses a number of existential risks, as powerful AI systems could pose a threat to humanity if they are not adequately managed. It is therefore essential that we develop responsible AI systems that are beneficial to humanity, and that we are constantly vigilant to potential risks. The implications of AI have been far-reaching, and it is clear that AI will continue to shape and transform human life and behavior in the years to come. It is therefore essential that we continue to develop responsible AI systems that are beneficial to humanity, and that we are constantly vigilant to potential risks.

Printed by Libri Plureos GmbH in Hamburg,
Germany